MASTERING JAVA

100+ Solved and Commented Exercises to Accelerate your Learning

MASTERING JAVA

100+ Solved and Commented Exercises to Accelerate your Learning

Ruhan Avila da Conceição

1st edition
ISBN: 9798856011929

Independently published
Kindle Direct Publishing
Amazon Inc.

Copyright Notice

Summary

Preface

Welcome to this book where solved and commented Java exercises are presented. In this book, you will find a collection of over 100 exercises designed to help you improve your programming skills in this powerful language.

Learning to program involves not only understanding theoretical concepts but also applying those concepts in real-life situations. That's exactly what you will find in this book: a wide variety of problems ranging from basic fundamentals to more complex challenges.

Each exercise is accompanied by a complete and detailed solution, which not only presents the source code but also explains the reasoning behind the approach taken. These comments discuss important concepts, provide valuable tips, and help understand how programming logic can be efficiently applied in problem-solving.

As you progress through the exercises, you will be challenged with tasks involving mathematical formula manipulation, strings, conditionals, loops, vector manipulation, matrices, and much more.

The main goal of this book is to provide a practical and comprehensive resource for programmers seeking improvement. Whether you are a beginner in Java looking to solidify your knowledge or an experienced programmer wishing to deepen your expertise, these exercises will serve as an excellent study guide and reference. This book is also suitable for teachers who would like to have a rich collection of solved Programming Logic exercises to create exercises and questions for their students.

In several exercises, multiple solutions are presented for the same proposed problem, involving different strategies and techniques.

Enjoy this learning journey and dive into the solved and commented Java exercises. Prepare yourself for stimulating challenges, creative solutions, and a unique opportunity to enhance your programming skills.

This book was written using artificial intelligence tools in content creation, but all materials have been reviewed and edited by the author to deliver a final high-quality product.

Happy reading, happy studying, and have fun exploring the fascinating world of Java programming

Ruhan Avila da Conceição.

Brief Introduction to Java

Java is a widely-used programming language expressly designed for use in the distributed environment of the internet. It was designed to have the "look and feel" of the C++ language, but it is simpler to use than C++ and enforces an object-oriented programming model.

Here are some key characteristics of Java:

Object-Oriented: In Java, everything is an Object. Java can be easily extended since it is based on the Object model.

Platform Independent: Unlike many other programming languages including C and C++, when Java is compiled, it is not compiled into platform-specific machine code, but into platform-independent byte code. This byte code is distributed over the web and interpreted by the Virtual Machine (JVM) on whichever platform it is being run on.

Simple: Java is designed to be easy to learn. If you understand the basic concept of OOP, Java would be easy to master.

Secure: With Java's secure feature, it enables to develop virus-free, tamper-free systems. Authentication techniques are based on public-key encryption.

Architectural-Neutral: Java compiler generates an architecture-neutral object file format, which makes the compiled code executable on many processors, with the presence of a Java runtime system.

Portable: Being architectural-neutral and having no implementation dependent aspects of the specification makes Java portable.

Robust: Java makes an effort to eliminate error-prone situations by emphasizing mainly on compile-time error checking and runtime checking.

Multithreaded: With Java's multithreaded feature, it is possible to write programs that can perform many tasks simultaneously.

Java was developed by James Gosling, a development leader in sun microsystem. Sun Microsystems in 1995. It was later acquired by Oracle Corporation.

Java is used in a wide variety of computing platforms from embedded devices and mobile phones to enterprise servers and supercomputers.

A basic structure of a Java program is shown below:

```java
public class Main {
    public static void main(String[] args) {
        System.out.println("Hello, World!");
    }
```

```
    }
```

This is a simple program that prints "*Hello, World!*" to the console. In the above example, ***public class Main*** is the declaration of the class. Java programs are made up of classes. The ***main*** method is the entry point of the program and ***System.out.println("Hello, World!");*** is the line which prints the text "*Hello, World!*" to the console.

Variables

In Java, a variable is a name given to a memory location. It's called a variable because the information stored in the memory location may change during the execution of the program. Each variable in Java has a specific data type, which determines the size and layout of the variable's memory, the range of values that can be stored within that memory, and the set of operations that can be applied to the variable.

There are three types of variables in Java:

Local Variables: A variable defined within a method is called a local variable. The variable will be destroyed once the method has completed.

Instance Variables (Non-static Fields): Instance variables are non-static and are declared in a class outside any method, constructor or block. They are created when an object is created with the use of the keyword 'new' and destroyed when the object is destroyed.

Class Variables (Static Fields): A variable that is declared as static is called a static variable. It cannot be local. There would only be one copy of each class variable per class, regardless of how many objects are created from it.

Java variable types are further divided into two groups:

Primitive Data Types: The primitive data types include boolean, char, byte, short, int, long, float and double.

Non-primitive Data Types (Reference/Object Data Types): Reference variables are created using defined constructors of the classes. They are used to access objects. These variables are declared to be of a specific type that cannot be changed. Class objects and various type of array variables come under reference data type.

Here is an example of how to declare variables in Java:

```java
public class Main {
  public static void main(String[] args) {
    String name = "John";   // String variable
    int age = 20;           // integer variable
    float mark = 85.5f;     // float variable
    char grade = 'A';       // character variable
    boolean passed = true;  // boolean variable
    System.out.println(name);
    System.out.println(age);
    System.out.println(mark);
    System.out.println(grade);
```

```
    System.out.println(passed);
  }
}
```

In this program, ***name***, ***age***, ***mark***, ***grade*** and ***passed*** are variables. ***String*** is a non-primitive data type whereas ***int***, ***float***, ***char*** and ***boolean*** are primitive data types.

Primitive Data Types

byte: The byte data type is an 8-bit signed two's complement integer. It has a minimum value of -128 and a maximum value of 127 (inclusive). The byte data type can be useful for saving memory in large arrays.

short: The short data type is a 16-bit signed two's complement integer. It has a minimum value of -32,768 and a maximum value of 32,767 (inclusive).

int: By default, the int data type is a 32-bit signed two's complement integer, which has a minimum value of $-(2^{31})$ and a maximum value of $2^{31}-1$.

long: The long data type is a 64-bit two's complement integer. The signed long has a minimum value of $-(2^{63})$ and a maximum value of $2^{63}-1$.

float: The float data type is a single-precision 32-bit IEEE 754 floating point. Use a float (instead of double) if you need to save memory in large arrays of floating point numbers.

double: The double data type is a double-precision 64-bit IEEE 754 floating point. For decimal values, this data type is generally the default choice.

boolean: The boolean data type has only two possible values: true and false. Use this data type for simple flags that track true/false conditions.

char: The char data type is a single 16-bit Unicode character. It has a minimum value of '\u0000' (or 0) and a maximum value of '\uffff' (or 65,535 inclusive).

Non-Primitive Data Types

Non-primitive data types are created by the programmer and are not defined by Java (except for String). Non-primitive types can be used to call methods to perform certain operations, while primitive types cannot. A non-primitive data type can also be null, while a primitive type cannot.

Examples of non-primitive types include Strings, Arrays, Classes, Interfaces, and so on. For example, String in Java is a non-primitive data type.

Printing data

Printing data to the console in Java is straightforward. You use ***System.out.print()*** or ***System.out.println()***.

Here's a brief explanation of the two methods:
- ***System.out.print()***: This method prints the text you pass to it, and the cursor remains at the end of the text in the console.
- ***System.out.println()***: This method prints the text you pass to it, and moves the cursor to the next line in the console. The '***ln***' in ***println*** stands for "***line.***"

Here are examples of using both methods:

```java
public class Main {
  public static void main(String[] args) {
    System.out.print("Hello, ");
    System.out.print("World!");

    System.out.println("Hello, ");
    System.out.println("World!");
  }
}
```

In this program, the **System.out.print** statements will output **Hello, World!** on the same line, while the **System.out.println** statements will output **Hello,** and **World!** on separate lines.

You can print all primitive data types, Strings, and even objects (which will be printed in a format defined by the class's **toString** method, unless you override it).

```java
public class Main {
  public static void main(String[] args) {
    int a = 10;
    double b = 20.5;
    boolean c = true;
    String d = "Hello, World!";

    System.out.println("The value of a: " + a);
    System.out.println("The value of b: " + b);
    System.out.println("The value of c: " + c);
    System.out.println("The value of d: " + d);
  }
}
```

In this program, we're declaring variables of different types, then printing them. The + operator is used to concatenate the string literal with the value of the variable.

Reading data

Java provides several ways to read user input. The **Scanner** class is one of the most commonly used ways to get user input from the standard input, which is typically the keyboard. The **Scanner** class is a part of the **java.util** package, so you'll need to import this package or the class itself before using it.

Here is an example of how you can use the **Scanner** class to read different types of input:

```java
import java.util.Scanner; // import the Scanner class
```

```java
public class Main {
  public static void main(String[] args) {
    Scanner scanner = new Scanner(System.in); // create a Scanner
object

    System.out.println("Enter your name:");
    String name = scanner.nextLine();  // read a whole line of input

    System.out.println("Enter your age:");
    int age = scanner.nextInt();  // read an integer input

    System.out.println("Enter your GPA:");
    double gpa = scanner.nextDouble();  // read a double input

    System.out.println("Your name is " + name);
    System.out.println("Your age is " + age);
    System.out.println("Your GPA is " + gpa);

    scanner.close();  // it's a good practice to close the scanner
when you're done
  }
}
```

In this program, we first import the **Scanner** class, then we create a **Scanner** object named **scanner**. We then use the **nextLine()**, **nextInt()**, and **nextDouble()** methods to read a String, an integer, and a double, respectively. Finally, we close the **Scanner** object using **scanner.close()** to prevent a resource leak.

It's worth noting that when using **scanner.nextInt()** or similar methods, it does not consume the last newline character from your input, and thus this newline is consumed in the next call to **nextLine()**. This might not be the desired behavior for your program, and it's generally a good idea to add an extra **nextLine()** call to consume the rest of the line when reading numeric or boolean data.

```java
import java.util.Scanner;

public class Main {
  public static void main(String[] args) {
    Scanner scanner = new Scanner(System.in);

    System.out.println("Enter your age:");
    int age = scanner.nextInt();
```

```
scanner.nextLine();   // consume the leftover newline

System.out.println("Enter your name:");
String name = scanner.nextLine();

System.out.println("Your name is " + name);
System.out.println("Your age is " + age);

scanner.close();
    }
}
```

In this program, we use **scanner.nextLine()** after **scanner.nextInt()** to consume the leftover newline.

Introduction to Exercises

If you have acquired this book, you want to start programming and be logically challenged as soon as possible, without wanting to read a sermon on the mount. But it is important to highlight a few things before we begin.

Even though many exercises may be considered easy, if you are new to this programming journey, it is important for you to first try to solve the problem on your own before looking at the solution. There is more than one possible solution to the same problem, and you need to think and develop your own solution. Then, you can compare it with the proposed one in the book, identify the strengths of each, and try to learn a little more.

If the exercise is too difficult and you can't solve it, move on to the next one and try again the next day. Don't immediately jump to the answer, even if you can't solve it, and definitely don't look at the answer without even attempting to solve it.

Learning programming logic is not about getting the answer; it's about the journey you take to arrive at the answer.

With that being said, the remaining chapters of this book are divided according to the programming topics covered in the proposed exercises

- Mathematical Formulas (15 exercises)
- Conditionals (20 exercises)
- Loop Structures (25 exercises)
- Arrays (10 exercises)
- Strings (10 exercises)
- Matrices (10 exercises)
- Recursive Functions (10 exercises)
- + Extra Exercises at the End

You can check out the complete list of exercises at the end of the book.

From now on, it's all up to you!

Mathematical Formulas

In Java, you can perform a variety of mathematical operations using operators and the built-in Math class.

Operators

The basic mathematical operators are:
+ for addition
- for subtraction
* for multiplication
/ for division
% for modulo (remainder of division)
Here is an example:

```java
public class Main {
  public static void main(String[] args) {
    int x = 10;
    int y = 20;

    int sum = x + y; // addition
    int diff = x - y; // subtraction
    int product = x * y; // multiplication
    int quotient = y / x; // division
    int remainder = y % x; // modulo

    System.out.println("Sum: " + sum);
    System.out.println("Difference: " + diff);
    System.out.println("Product: " + product);
    System.out.println("Quotient: " + quotient);
    System.out.println("Remainder: " + remainder);
  }
}
```

Math class

Java provides the **Math** class in the java.util package which has several methods that can be used for mathematical operations. These include:
Math.abs(number): returns the absolute value of the number.

Math.max(number1, number2): returns the maximum of two numbers.

Math.min(number1, number2): returns the minimum of two numbers.

Math.sqrt(number): returns the square root of the number.

Math.cbrt(number): returns the cube root of the number.

Math.pow(number, power): returns the value of the first parameter raised to the second parameter.

Math.round(number): returns the number rounded to the nearest whole number.

Math.ceil(number): rounds a number UP to the nearest integer, if necessary, and returns the result.

Math.floor(number): rounds a number DOWN to the nearest integer, if necessary, and returns the result.

Here's an example of how to use the Math class:

```
public class Main {
  public static void main(String[] args) {
    double x = 10.6;
    double y = 20.5;

    System.out.println("Max: " + Math.max(x, y));
    System.out.println("Min: " + Math.min(x, y));
    System.out.println("Square root of y: " + Math.sqrt(y));
    System.out.println("y to the power of x: " + Math.pow(y, x));
    System.out.println("Round of y: " + Math.round(y));
    System.out.println("Ceiling of x: " + Math.ceil(x));
    System.out.println("Floor of x: " + Math.floor(x));
  }
}
```

1. Write a program that prompts the user for two numbers and displays the addition, subtraction, multiplication, and division between them.

```
public class ArithmeticCalculator {
    public static void main(String[] args) {
        // Create a Scanner object to read input from the user
        Scanner scanner = new Scanner(System.in);

        // Prompt the user for the first number
        System.out.print("Enter the first number: ");
        double num1 = scanner.nextDouble();

        // Prompt the user for the second number
```

```java
        System.out.print("Enter the second number: ");
        double num2 = scanner.nextDouble();

        // Perform arithmetic operations
        double addition = num1 + num2;
        double subtraction = num1 - num2;
        double multiplication = num1 * num2;
        double division = num1 / num2;

        // Display the results
        System.out.println("Addition: " + addition);
        System.out.println("Subtraction: " + subtraction);
        System.out.println("Multiplication: " + multiplication);
        System.out.println("Division: " + division);

        // Close the Scanner
        scanner.close();
    }
}
```

We begin by importing the ***java.util.Scanner*** class, which allows us to read user input from the console.

We define the ***ArithmeticCalculator*** class, which will contain our ***main*** method.

Inside the ***main*** method, we create a ***Scanner*** object named ***scanner*** to read input from the user.

We use ***System.out.print*** and ***scanner.nextDouble()*** to prompt the user to enter the first number. The entered value is then stored in the variable ***num1***.

Similarly, we prompt the user to enter the second number using ***System.out.print*** and ***scanner.nextDouble()***, and store the entered value in the variable ***num2***.

Next, we perform the four arithmetic operations using the entered numbers: addition (***num1 + num2***), subtraction (***num1 - num2***), multiplication (***num1 * num2***), and division (***num1 / num2***). The results of these operations are stored in separate variables: ***addition***, ***subtraction***, ***multiplication***, and ***division***.

Finally, we use ***System.out.println*** to display the results of the arithmetic operations to the user.

We close the ***Scanner*** object to free up system resources using the ***scanner.close()*** method.

2. Write a program that calculates the arithmetic mean of two numbers.

```java
import java.util.Scanner;

public class ArithmeticMeanCalculator {
    public static void main(String[] args) {
        // Create a Scanner object to read input from the user
        Scanner scanner = new Scanner(System.in);

        // Prompt the user for the first number
        System.out.print("Enter the first number: ");
        double num1 = scanner.nextDouble();

        // Prompt the user for the second number
        System.out.print("Enter the second number: ");
        double num2 = scanner.nextDouble();

        // Calculate the arithmetic mean
        double arithmeticMean = (num1 + num2) / 2;

        // Display the arithmetic mean
        System.out.println("Arithmetic Mean: " + arithmeticMean);

        // Close the Scanner
        scanner.close();
    }
}
```

We import the *java.util.Scanner* class to read user input.

We define the *ArithmeticMeanCalculator* class, which will contain our *main* method.

Inside the *main* method, we create a *Scanner* object named *scanner* to read input from the user.

We use *System.out.print* and *scanner.nextDouble()* to prompt the user to enter the first number. The entered value is then stored in the variable *num1*.

Similarly, we prompt the user to enter the second number using *System.out.print* and *scanner.nextDouble()*, and store the entered value in the variable *num2*.

Next, we calculate the arithmetic mean of the two numbers using the formula: *(num1 + num2) / 2*, and store the result in the variable *arithmeticMean*.

Finally, we use *System.out.println* to display the arithmetic mean to the user.

We close the ***Scanner*** object to free up system resources using the **scanner.close()** method.

3. Create a program that calculates and displays the arithmetic mean of three grades entered by the user.

```java
import java.util.Scanner;

public class GradeAverageCalculator {
    public static void main(String[] args) {
        // Create a Scanner object to read input from the user
        Scanner scanner = new Scanner(System.in);

        // Prompt the user for the three grades
        System.out.print("Enter the first grade: ");
        double grade1 = scanner.nextDouble();

        System.out.print("Enter the second grade: ");
        double grade2 = scanner.nextDouble();

        System.out.print("Enter the third grade: ");
        double grade3 = scanner.nextDouble();

        // Calculate the arithmetic mean
        double arithmeticMean = (grade1 + grade2 + grade3) / 3;

        // Display the arithmetic mean
        System.out.println("Arithmetic Mean of the three grades: " +
 arithmeticMean);

        // Close the Scanner
        scanner.close();
    }
}
```

We begin by importing the ***java.util.Scanner*** class, which allows us to read user input from the console. This class is part of the Java standard library and makes it easy to handle user input.

Next, we define the ***GradeAverageCalculator*** class, which will contain our main method.

Inside the ***main*** method, we create a ***Scanner*** object named ***scanner*** to read input from the user. We use this object to obtain the user's grades.

We prompt the user to enter the first grade using ***System.out.print*** and **scanner.nextDouble()**. The entered value is then stored in the variable ***grade1***.

Similarly, we prompt the user to enter the second grade and store the entered value in the variable **grade2**. We then prompt the user to enter the third grade and store the entered value in the variable **grade3**.

Next, we calculate the arithmetic mean of the three grades using the formula: **(grade1 + grade2 + grade3) / 3**. We add up the three grades and divide the sum by 3 to get the average.

Finally, we use **System.out.println** to display the calculated arithmetic mean to the user.

We close the **Scanner** object to free up system resources using the **scanner.close()** method. This step is essential to prevent resource leaks and should be done when we are done using the **Scanner**.

4. Write a program that calculates the geometric mean of three numbers entered by the user

```java
import java.util.Scanner;

public class GeometricMeanCalculator {
    public static void main(String[] args) {
        // Create a Scanner object to read input from the user
        Scanner scanner = new Scanner(System.in);

        // Prompt the user to enter the three numbers
        System.out.print("Enter the first number: ");
        double num1 = scanner.nextDouble();

        System.out.print("Enter the second number: ");
        double num2 = scanner.nextDouble();

        System.out.print("Enter the third number: ");
        double num3 = scanner.nextDouble();

        // Calculate the geometric mean
        double geometricMean = Math.pow(num1 * num2 * num3, 1.0 /
3.0);

        // Display the geometric mean
        System.out.println("Geometric Mean: " + geometricMean);

        // Close the Scanner
        scanner.close();
    }
}
```

22

We begin by importing the *java.util.Scanner* class, which allows us to read user input from the console. This class is part of the Java standard library and makes it easy to handle user input.

Next, we define the *GeometricMeanCalculator* class, which will contain our *main* method.

Inside the *main* method, we create a *Scanner* object named *scanner* to read input from the user. We use this object to obtain the three numbers.

We prompt the user to enter the first number using *System.out.print* and *scanner.nextDouble()*. The entered value is then stored in the variable *num1*.

Similarly, we prompt the user to enter the second number and store the entered value in the variable *num2*.

We then prompt the user to enter the third number and store the entered value in the variable *num3*.

Next, we calculate the geometric mean of the three numbers using the formula: *geometricMean = cubeRoot(num1 * num2 * num3)*. We can find the geometric mean by multiplying the three numbers together and then taking the cube root of the product. We use the *Math.pow* method to calculate the cube root, as it's equivalent to raising to the power of *1.0 / 3.0*.

Finally, we use *System.out.println* to display the calculated geometric mean to the user.

We close the *Scanner* object to free up system resources using the *scanner.close()* method. This step is essential to prevent resource leaks and should be done when we are done using the *Scanner*.

5. Write a program that calculates the BMI of an individual, using the formula BMI = weight / height²

```java
import java.util.Scanner;

public class BMICalculator {
    public static void main(String[] args) {
        // Create a Scanner object to read input from the user
        Scanner scanner = new Scanner(System.in);

        // Prompt the user to enter weight in kilograms
        System.out.print("Enter your weight in kilograms: ");
        double weight = scanner.nextDouble();

        // Prompt the user to enter height in meters
        System.out.print("Enter your height in meters: ");
        double height = scanner.nextDouble();

        // Calculate BMI
        double bmi = weight / (height * height);
```

```
    // Display the BMI
    System.out.println("Your BMI is: " + bmi);

    // Close the Scanner
    scanner.close();
    }
}
```

We start by importing the *java.util.Scanner* class, which allows us to read user input from the console. This class is part of the Java standard library and makes it easy to handle user input.

Next, we define the *BMICalculator* class, which will contain our main method.

Inside the *main* method, we create a *Scanner* object named scanner to read input from the user. We use this object to obtain the user's weight and height.

We prompt the user to enter their weight in kilograms using *System.out.print* and *scanner.nextDouble()*. The entered value is then stored in the variable *weight*.

Similarly, we prompt the user to enter their height in meters and store the entered value in the variable *height*.

Next, we calculate the BMI using the formula: *BMI = weight / (height * height)*. We divide the *weight* by the square of the *height* (*height * height*) to get the BMI.

Finally, we use *System.out.println* to display the calculated BMI to the user.

We close the *Scanner* object to free up system resources using the *scanner.close()* method. This step is essential to prevent resource leaks and should be done when we are done using the *Scanner*.

When you run this Java program, it will prompt you to enter your weight and height in kilograms and meters, respectively. After you provide the input, it will calculate and display your BMI.

6. Create a program that calculates and displays the perimeter of a circle, prompting the user for the radius.

```
import java.util.Scanner;

public class CirclePerimeterCalculator {
    public static void main(String[] args) {
        // Create a Scanner object to read input from the user
        Scanner scanner = new Scanner(System.in);

        // Prompt the user to enter the radius of the circle
```

```java
        System.out.print("Enter the radius of the circle: ");
        double radius = scanner.nextDouble();

        // Calculate the perimeter of the circle
        double perimeter = 2 * Math.PI * radius;

        // Display the perimeter of the circle
        System.out.println("Perimeter of the circle: " + perimeter);

        // Close the Scanner
        scanner.close();
    }
}
```

We start by importing the ***java.util.Scanner*** class, which allows us to read user input from the console. This class is part of the Java standard library and makes it easy to handle user input.

Next, we define the ***CirclePerimeterCalculator*** class, which will contain our main method.

Inside the ***main*** method, we create a ***Scanner*** object named ***scanner*** to read input from the user. We use this object to obtain the user's input (radius of the circle).

We prompt the user to enter the radius of the circle using ***System.out.print*** and ***scanner.nextDouble()***. The entered value is then stored in the variable ***radius***.

Next, we calculate the perimeter of the circle using the formula: ***perimeter = 2 * π * radius***. We use ***Math.PI*** to get the value of π (approximately 3.14159) from the Java standard library. The formula calculates the distance around the circle, which is the perimeter.

Finally, we use ***System.out.println*** to display the calculated perimeter of the circle to the user.

We close the ***Scanner*** object to free up system resources using the ***scanner.close()*** method. This step is essential to prevent resource leaks and should be done when we are done using the ***Scanner***.

7. Write a program that calculates the area of a circle from the radius, using the formula A = πr^2

```java
import java.util.Scanner;

public class CircleAreaCalculator {
    public static void main(String[] args) {
        // Create a Scanner object to read input from the user
        Scanner scanner = new Scanner(System.in);
```

```java
        // Prompt the user to enter the radius of the circle
        System.out.print("Enter the radius of the circle: ");
        double radius = scanner.nextDouble();

        // Calculate the area of the circle
        double area = Math.PI * Math.pow(radius, 2);

        // Display the area of the circle
        System.out.println("Area of the circle: " + area);

        // Close the Scanner
        scanner.close();
    }
}
```

We start by importing the **java.util.Scanner** class, which allows us to read user input from the console. This class is part of the Java standard library and makes it easy to handle user input.

Next, we define the **CircleAreaCalculator** class, which will contain our main method.

Inside the **main** method, we create a **Scanner** object named **scanner** to read input from the user. We use this object to obtain the user's input (radius of the circle).

We prompt the user to enter the radius of the circle using **System.out.print** and **scanner.nextDouble()**. The entered value is then stored in the variable **radius**.

Next, we calculate the area of the circle using the formula: **area = π * radius²**. We use **Math.PI** to get the value of π (approximately 3.14159) from the Java standard library, and **Math.pow** to calculate the square of the radius.

Finally, we use **System.out.println** to display the calculated area of the circle to the user.

We close the **Scanner** object to free up system resources using the **scanner.close()** method. This step is essential to prevent resource leaks and should be done when we are done using the **Scanner**.

8. Write a program that calculates the delta of a quadratic equation ($\Delta = b^2 - 4ac$).

```java
import java.util.Scanner;

public class QuadraticDeltaCalculator {
    public static void main(String[] args) {
        // Create a Scanner object to read input from the user
        Scanner scanner = new Scanner(System.in);
```

```java
        // Prompt the user to enter the coefficients a, b, and c
        System.out.print("Enter the coefficient a: ");
        double a = scanner.nextDouble();

        System.out.print("Enter the coefficient b: ");
        double b = scanner.nextDouble();

        System.out.print("Enter the coefficient c: ");
        double c = scanner.nextDouble();

        // Calculate the delta (Δ) of the quadratic equation
        double delta = Math.pow(b, 2) - 4 * a * c;

        // Display the delta of the quadratic equation
        System.out.println("Delta (Δ) of the quadratic equation: "
 + delta);

        // Close the Scanner
        scanner.close();
    }
 }
```

We start by importing the ***java.util.Scanner*** class, which allows us to read user input from the console. This class is part of the Java standard library and makes it easy to handle user input.

Next, we define the ***QuadraticDeltaCalculator*** class, which will contain our main method.

Inside the ***main*** method, we create a ***Scanner*** object named scanner to read input from the user. We use this object to obtain the user's input (coefficients ***a***, ***b***, and ***c*** of the quadratic equation).

We prompt the user to enter the coefficients a, b, and c of the quadratic equation using ***System.out.print*** and ***scanner.nextDouble()***. The entered values are then stored in variables ***a***, ***b***, and ***c***, respectively.

Next, we calculate the delta (Δ) of the quadratic equation using the formula: $\Delta = b^2 - 4ac$. We use ***Math.pow*** to calculate the square of ***b***, and standard arithmetic operations to perform the rest of the calculations.

Finally, we use ***System.out.println*** to display the calculated delta (Δ) of the quadratic equation to the user.

We close the ***Scanner*** object to free up system resources using the ***scanner.close()*** method. This step is essential to prevent resource leaks and should be done when we are done using the ***Scanner***.

9. Write a program that calculates the perimeter and area of a rectangle, using the formulas P = 2(w + l) and A = wl, where w is the width and l is the length

```java
import java.util.Scanner;

public class RectangleCalculator {
    public static void main(String[] args) {
        // Create a Scanner object to read input from the user
        Scanner scanner = new Scanner(System.in);

        // Prompt the user to enter the width of the rectangle
        System.out.print("Enter the width of the rectangle: ");
        double width = scanner.nextDouble();

        // Prompt the user to enter the length of the rectangle
        System.out.print("Enter the length of the rectangle: ");
        double length = scanner.nextDouble();

        // Calculate the perimeter of the rectangle
        double perimeter = 2 * (width + length);

        // Calculate the area of the rectangle
        double area = width * length;

        // Display the perimeter and area of the rectangle
        System.out.println("Perimeter of the rectangle: " +
perimeter);
        System.out.println("Area of the rectangle: " + area);

        // Close the Scanner
        scanner.close();
    }
}
```

We start by importing the ***java.util.Scanner*** class, which allows us to read user input from the console. This class is part of the Java standard library and makes it easy to handle user input.

Next, we define the ***RectangleCalculator*** class, which will contain our main method.

Inside the ***main*** method, we create a ***Scanner*** object named scanner to read input from the user. We use this object to obtain the user's input (width and length of the rectangle).

We prompt the user to enter the width of the rectangle using **System.out.print** and **scanner.nextDouble()**. The entered value is then stored in the variable **width**.

Similarly, we prompt the user to enter the length of the rectangle and store the entered value in the variable **length**.

Next, we calculate the perimeter of the rectangle using the formula: **perimeter = 2 * (width + length)**. We add the width and length together, and then multiply the sum by 2 to get the perimeter.

Similarly, we calculate the area of the rectangle using the formula: **area = width * length**. We simply multiply the width and length together to get the area.

Finally, we use **System.out.println** to display the calculated perimeter and area of the rectangle to the user.

We close the **Scanner** object to free up system resources using the **scanner.close()** method. This step is essential to prevent resource leaks and should be done when we are done using the **Scanner**.

10. Write a program that calculates the perimeter and area of a triangle, using the formulas P = a + b + c and A = (b * h) / 2, where a, b and c are the sides of the triangle and h is the height relative to the side B.

```java
import java.util.Scanner;

public class TriangleCalculator {
    public static void main(String[] args) {
        // Create a Scanner object to read input from the user
        Scanner scanner = new Scanner(System.in);

        // Prompt the user to enter the sides of the triangle
        System.out.print("Enter the side a of the triangle: ");
        double a = scanner.nextDouble();

        System.out.print("Enter the side b of the triangle: ");
        double b = scanner.nextDouble();

        System.out.print("Enter the side c of the triangle: ");
        double c = scanner.nextDouble();

        // Prompt the user to enter the height relative to side B
        System.out.print("Enter the height relative to side B: ");
        double h = scanner.nextDouble();

        // Calculate the perimeter of the triangle
```

```java
        double perimeter = a + b + c;

        // Calculate the area of the triangle
        double area = (b * h) / 2;

        // Display the perimeter and area of the triangle
        System.out.println("Perimeter of the triangle: " +
perimeter);
        System.out.println("Area of the triangle: " + area);

        // Close the Scanner
        scanner.close();
    }
}
```

We start by importing the *java.util.Scanner* class, which allows us to read user input from the console. This class is part of the Java standard library and makes it easy to handle user input.

Next, we define the *TriangleCalculator* class, which will contain our main method.

Inside the *main* method, we create a *Scanner* object named *scanner* to read input from the user. We use this object to obtain the user's input (sides *a*, *b*, *c*, and height *h* of the triangle).

We prompt the user to enter the sides *a*, *b*, and *c* of the triangle using *System.out.print* and *scanner.nextDouble()*. The entered values are then stored in variables *a*, *b*, and *c*.

Next, we prompt the user to enter the height *h* relative to side B using *System.out.print* and *scanner.nextDouble()*. The entered value is then stored in the variable *h*.

Now, we calculate the perimeter of the triangle using the formula: *perimeter = a + b + c*. We add the three sides together to get the perimeter.

Similarly, we calculate the area of the triangle using the formula: *area = (b * h) / 2*. We multiply side B (*b*) by the height (*h*) and then divide the product by 2 to get the area.

Finally, we use *System.out.println* to display the calculated perimeter and area of the triangle to the user.

We close the *Scanner* object to free up system resources using the *scanner.close()* method. This step is essential to prevent resource leaks and should be done when we are done using the *Scanner*.

11. Write a program that calculates the average velocity of an object, using the formula v = Δs/Δt, where v is the average velocity, Δs is the space variation, and Δt is the time variation

```java
import java.util.Scanner;
```

```java
public class AverageVelocityCalculator {
    public static void main(String[] args) {
        // Create a Scanner object to read input from the user
        Scanner scanner = new Scanner(System.in);

        // Prompt the user to enter the space variation (Δs)
        System.out.print("Enter the space variation (Δs) in meters:
");
        double spaceVariation = scanner.nextDouble();

        // Prompt the user to enter the time variation (Δt)
        System.out.print("Enter the time variation (Δt) in seconds:
");
        double timeVariation = scanner.nextDouble();

        // Calculate the average velocity (v)
        double averageVelocity = spaceVariation / timeVariation;

        // Display the average velocity
        System.out.println("Average velocity: " + averageVelocity +
" meters per second");

        // Close the Scanner
        scanner.close();
    }
}
```

We start by importing the ***java.util.Scanner*** class, which allows us to read user input from the console. This class is part of the Java standard library and makes it easy to handle user input.

Next, we define the ***AverageVelocityCalculator*** class, which will contain our main method.

Inside the ***main*** method, we create a ***Scanner*** object named ***scanner*** to read input from the user. We use this object to obtain the user's input for the space variation (Δs) and the time variation (Δt).

We prompt the user to enter the space variation (Δs) in meters using ***System.out.print*** and ***scanner.nextDouble()***. The entered value is then stored in the variable ***spaceVariation***. Similarly, we prompt the user to enter the time variation (Δt) in seconds using ***System.out.print*** and ***scanner.nextDouble()***. The entered value is then stored in the variable ***timeVariation***.

Next, we calculate the average velocity of the object using the formula: ***averageVelocity*** = ***Δs*** / ***Δt***. We divide the space variation (*spaceVariation*) by the time variation (*timeVariation*) to get the average velocity.

Finally, we use ***System.out.println*** to display the calculated average velocity of the object to the user in meters per second.

We close the ***Scanner*** object to free up system resources using the ***scanner.close()*** method. This step is essential to prevent resource leaks and should be done when we are done using the ***Scanner***.

12. Write a program that calculates the kinetic energy of a moving object, using the formula E = (mv²) / 2, where E is the kinetic energy, m is the mass of the object, and v is the velocity.

```java
import java.util.Scanner;

public class KineticEnergyCalculator {
    public static void main(String[] args) {
        // Create a Scanner object to read input from the user
        Scanner scanner = new Scanner(System.in);

        // Prompt the user to enter the mass of the object
        System.out.print("Enter the mass of the object (in
kilograms): ");
        double mass = scanner.nextDouble();

        // Prompt the user to enter the velocity of the object
        System.out.print("Enter the velocity of the object (in
meters per second): ");
        double velocity = scanner.nextDouble();

        // Calculate the kinetic energy (E) of the object
        double kineticEnergy = (mass * Math.pow(velocity, 2)) / 2;

        // Display the kinetic energy of the object
        System.out.println("Kinetic energy of the object: " +
kineticEnergy + " joules");

        // Close the Scanner
        scanner.close();
    }
}
```

In this program, we prompt the user to enter the mass of the object (in kilograms) and the velocity of the object (in meters per second). The entered values are then stored in variables ***mass*** and ***velocity***, respectively. We calculate the kinetic energy (E - *kineticEnergy*) of the object using the formula: ***kineticEnergy = (mass * velocity^2) / 2***. We use ***Math.pow*** to calculate the square of the velocity. The kinetic energy is a measure of the energy an object possesses due to its motion.

Finally, we display the calculated kinetic energy of the object to the user in joules.

13. Write a program that calculates the work done by a force acting on an object, using the formula W = F * d, where W is the work, F is the applied force, and d is the distance traveled by the object.

```java
import java.util.Scanner;

public class WorkCalculator {
    public static void main(String[] args) {
        // Create a Scanner object to read input from the user
        Scanner scanner = new Scanner(System.in);

        // Prompt the user to enter the applied force (F) in newtons
        System.out.print("Enter the applied force (F) in newtons: ");
        double force = scanner.nextDouble();

        // Prompt the user to enter the distance traveled (d) by the
object in meters
        System.out.print("Enter the distance traveled (d) by the
object in meters: ");
        double distance = scanner.nextDouble();

        // Calculate the work done (T) by the force on the object
        double work = force * distance;

        // Display the work done by the force on the object
        System.out.println("Work done by the force on the object: "
+ work + " joules");

        // Close the Scanner
        scanner.close();
    }
}
```

In this program, we prompt the user to enter the applied force (F) in newtons and the distance traveled (d) by the object in meters. The entered values are then stored in variables ***force*** and ***distance***, respectively. We then calculate the work done using the provided formula $W = F * d \Rightarrow \textbf{work} = \textbf{force} * \textbf{distance}$. Finally, we display the calculated work done by the force on the object to the user in joules.

14. Write a program that reads the x and y position of two points in the Cartesian plane, and calculates the distance between them.

```java
import java.util.Scanner;

public class DistanceCalculator {
    public static void main(String[] args) {
        // Create a Scanner object to read input from the user
        Scanner scanner = new Scanner(System.in);

        // Prompt the user to enter the x and y coordinates of the
first point
        System.out.print("Enter the x-coordinate of the first point:
");
        double x1 = scanner.nextDouble();
        System.out.print("Enter the y-coordinate of the first point:
");
        double y1 = scanner.nextDouble();

        // Prompt the user to enter the x and y coordinates of the
second point
        System.out.print("Enter the x-coordinate of the second
point: ");
        double x2 = scanner.nextDouble();
        System.out.print("Enter the y-coordinate of the second
point: ");
        double y2 = scanner.nextDouble();

        // Calculate the distance between the two points using the
distance formula
        double distance = Math.sqrt(Math.pow(x2 - x1, 2) +
Math.pow(y2 - y1, 2));

        // Display the distance between the two points
        System.out.println("Distance between the two points: " +
distance);

        // Close the Scanner
```

```
            scanner.close();
    }
}
```

We start by importing the ***java.util.Scanner*** class, which allows us to read user input from the console. This class is part of the Java standard library and makes it easy to handle user input.

Next, we define the ***DistanceCalculator*** class, which will contain our main method.

Inside the ***main*** method, we create a ***Scanner*** object named ***scanner*** to read input from the user. We use this object to obtain the user's input for the x and y coordinates of both points.

We prompt the user to enter the x and y coordinates of the first point using ***System.out.print*** and ***scanner.nextDouble()***. The entered values are then stored in variables ***x1*** and ***y1***.

Similarly, we prompt the user to enter the x and y coordinates of the second point using ***System.out.print*** and ***scanner.nextDouble()***. The entered values are then stored in variables ***x2*** and ***y2***.

Next, we calculate the distance between the two points using the distance formula: $d = \sqrt{(x2 - x1)^2 + (y2 - y1)^2}$

We use ***Math.sqrt*** to calculate the square root of the sum of the squares of the differences in the x and y coordinates. This formula gives us the Euclidean distance between two points in a two-dimensional Cartesian plane.

Finally, we use ***System.out.println*** to display the calculated distance between the two points to the user.

15. Create a program that prompts the user for the radius of a sphere and calculates and displays its volume.

```java
import java.util.Scanner;

public class SphereVolumeCalculator {
    public static void main(String[] args) {
        // Create a Scanner object to read input from the user
        Scanner scanner = new Scanner(System.in);

        // Prompt the user to enter the radius of the sphere
        System.out.print("Enter the radius of the sphere: ");
        double radius = scanner.nextDouble();

        // Calculate the volume of the sphere
        double volume = (4.0 / 3.0) * Math.PI * Math.pow(radius, 3);

        // Display the volume of the sphere
```

```
System.out.println("Volume of the sphere: " + volume);

        // Close the Scanner
        scanner.close();
    }
}
```

In this program, we prompt the user to enter the radius of the sphere. The entered value is then stored in the variable **radius**. We then calculate the volume of the sphere using the provided formula $V = (4/3) * \pi * r^3$, where π is the mathematical constant representing pi (approximately 3.14159), and r^3 means the radius raised to the power of 3. To calculate the volume, we use the **Math.pow()** method to raise the radius to the power of 3, and then we multiply it with **4.0 / 3.0** and **Math.PI**, which gives us the volume of the sphere.

Finally, we display the calculated volume of the sphere to the user.

Conditionals

Before moving on to the exercises and their respective commented solutions, let's make an introduction to some important content for solving the activities.

Comparison Operators

Comparison operators are used to compare two values in Java. These operators can be used with many types of values, including integers, floating-point numbers, and strings.

All of these operators return a boolean result either ***true*** or ***false*** and are often used in conditional statements like ***if, while, do-while***, etc.

Here are the comparison operators in Java:

<u>Equal to *(==)*</u>: Checks if two values are equal.

```
int x = 5;
if (x == 5) {
  System.out.println("x is 5");
}
```

<u>Not equal to *(!=)*</u>: Checks if two values are not equal.

```
int x = 5;
if (x != 10) {
  System.out.println("x is not 10");
}
```

<u>Greater than *(>)*</u>: Checks if the left operand is greater than the right operand.

```
int x = 5;
if (x > 3) {
  System.out.println("x is greater than 3");
}
```

<u>Less than *(<)*</u>: Checks if the left operand is less than the right operand.

```
int x = 5;
if (x < 10) {
  System.out.println("x is less than 10");
}
```

Greater than or equal to (>=): Checks if the left operand is greater than or equal to the right operand.

```
int x = 5;
if (x >= 5) {
    System.out.println("x is greater than or equal to 5");
}
```

Less than or equal to (<=): Checks if the left operand is less than or equal to the right operand.

```
int x = 5;
if (x <= 5) {
    System.out.println("x is less than or equal to 5");
}
```

Logical Operators

In Java, there are three main logical operators: and (&&), or (||) and not (!). These operators are used to combine logical expressions and evaluate complex conditions. Here is a detailed explanation of each operator:

and operator - **&&**:

The and operator is used to combine two or more logical expressions. It returns **true** only if all expressions are **true**. Otherwise, it returns **false**. The truth table for the and operator is as follows:

x	y	x && y
true	true	true
true	false	false
false	true	false
false	false	false

```
int x = 5;
if (x > 0 && x < 10) {
    System.out.println("x is a positive single digit number.");
}
```

or operator:

The **or** operator is used to combine two or more logical expressions. It returns **True** if at least one of the expressions is true. Returns **False** only if all expressions are false. The truth table for the or operator is as follows:

38

x	y	x || y
True	True	True
True	False	True
False	True	True
False	False	False

```java
int x = 5;
if (x < 0 || x > 4) {
   System.out.println("x is either negative or greater than 4.");
}
```

not operator:

The **not** operator is used to negate a logical expression. It reverses the value of the expression. If the expression is **True**, the **not** operator returns **False**. If the expression is **False**, the not operator returns **True**.

```java
boolean isCold = false;
if (!isCold) {
   System.out.println("It's not cold today.");
}
```

It's important to note that **&&** and **||** are short-circuit operators. This means that they only evaluate the right-hand operand if it's necessary to determine the result.

For instance, if **A** and **B** are two operands, then:

In the case of **A && B**, if **A** is *false*, Java won't evaluate **B**, because the result of the AND operation will be *false* regardless of the value of **B**.

In the case of **A || B**, if **A** is *true*, Java won't evaluate **B**, because the result of the OR operation will be *true* regardless of the value of **B**.

This feature can be used to prevent errors during runtime (for example, checking for a null reference before accessing an object's methods or properties), and can also improve performance by avoiding unnecessary calculations.

Conditionals in Java

Conditional statements in Java allow your program to make decisions based on certain conditions. Here are the main types of conditional statements in Java:

if statement: The most basic control flow statement supported by Java is the if statement.

```
int num = 10;
if (num > 5) {
   System.out.println("Number is greater than 5");
}
```

if-else statement: The if statement alone will execute a block of code if, and only if, a condition is true. The if-else statement allows you to execute a block of code if the condition is true and another block if it is false.

```
int num = 4;
if (num > 5) {
   System.out.println("Number is greater than 5");
} else {
   System.out.println("Number is not greater than 5");
}
```

else if statement: If you have multiple conditions to check, you can use else if for this.

```
int num = 25;
if (num > 30) {
   System.out.println("Number is greater than 30");
} else if (num > 20) {
   System.out.println("Number is greater than 20");
} else {
   System.out.println("Number is not greater than 20");
}
```

switch statement: A ***switch*** statement allows a variable to be tested for equality against a list of values. Each value is called a case, and the variable being switched on is checked for each switch case.

```
int day = 3;
switch (day) {
   case 1:
      System.out.println("Monday");
      break;
   case 2:
      System.out.println("Tuesday");
      break;
   case 3:
      System.out.println("Wednesday");
      break;
   // You can have any number of case statements.
   default: // Optional
```

```
        System.out.println("Invalid day");
    }
```

In this **switch** statement example, if the **day** variable matches any case, the corresponding code block will be executed. The **break** statement is used to terminate the current case and move on to the next one. If no case matches, the code under **default** will be executed.

16. Make a program that asks for a person's age and displays whether they are of legal age or not.

```java
import java.util.Scanner;

public class LegalAgeChecker {
    public static void main(String[] args) {
        // Create a Scanner object to read input from the user
        Scanner scanner = new Scanner(System.in);

        // Prompt the user to enter their age
        System.out.print("Enter your age: ");
        int age = scanner.nextInt();

        // Check if the person is of legal age (age >= 18)
        boolean isLegalAge = age >= 18;

        // Display the result based on whether the person is of
legal age or not
        if (isLegalAge) {
            System.out.println("You are of legal age.");
        } else {
            System.out.println("You are not of legal age.");
        }

        // Close the Scanner
        scanner.close();
    }
}
```

We start by importing the **java.util.Scanner** class, which allows us to read user input from the console. This class is part of the Java standard library and makes it easy to handle user input.

Next, we define the **LegalAgeChecker** class, which will contain our main method.

Inside the **main** method, we create a **Scanner** object named **scanner** to read input from the user. We use this object to obtain the user's input for their age.

We prompt the user to enter their age using **System.out.print** and **scanner.nextInt()**. The entered value is then stored in the variable **age**.

We use a boolean variable **isLegalAge** to check if the person is of legal age. We do this by comparing the **age** with the legal age threshold, which is 18 in this case. If the **age** is greater than or equal to 18, then **isLegalAge** will be **true**, indicating that the person is of legal age. Otherwise, it will be **false**, indicating that the person is not of legal age.

Finally, we use an **if-else** statement to display the appropriate message based on whether the person is of legal age or not. If **isLegalAge** is **true**, it means the person is of legal age, so we display "*You are of legal age.*" If **isLegalAge** is **false**, it means the person is not of legal age, so we display "*You are not of legal age.*"

We close the **Scanner** object to free up system resources using the **scanner.close()** method. This step is essential to prevent resource leaks and should be done when we are done using the **Scanner**.

17. Write a program that reads two numbers and tells you which one is bigger.

```java
import java.util.Scanner;

public class BiggerNumberChecker {
    public static void main(String[] args) {
        // Create a Scanner object to read input from the user
        Scanner scanner = new Scanner(System.in);

        // Prompt the user to enter the first number
        System.out.print("Enter the first number: ");
        double number1 = scanner.nextDouble();

        // Prompt the user to enter the second number
        System.out.print("Enter the second number: ");
        double number2 = scanner.nextDouble();

        // Check which number is bigger using an if statement
        if (number1 > number2) {
            System.out.println("The bigger number is: " + number1);
        } else if (number2 > number1) {
            System.out.println("The bigger number is: " + number2);
        } else {
            System.out.println("Both numbers are equal.");
```

```
        }

        // Close the Scanner
        scanner.close();
    }
}
```

Inside the **main** method, we create a **Scanner** object named **scanner** to read input from the user. We use this object to obtain the user's input for the two numbers.

We prompt the user to enter the first number using **System.out.print** and **scanner.nextDouble()**. The entered value is then stored in the variable **number1**.

Similarly, we prompt the user to enter the second number using **System.out.print** and **scanner.nextDouble()**. The entered value is then stored in the variable **number2**.

We use an **if** statement to compare the two numbers and determine which one is bigger.

- If **number1** is greater than **number2**, the condition **number1 > number2** evaluates to **true**, and the code inside the **if** block will be executed. It means **number1** is bigger than **number2**, so we display "*The bigger number is:* " followed by **number1**.
- If **number2** is greater than **number1**, the condition **number2 > number1** evaluates to **true**, and the code inside the **else if** block will be executed. It means **number2** is bigger than **number1**, so we display "*The bigger number is:* " followed by **number2**.
- If both numbers are equal, none of the above conditions will be **true**, and the code inside the **else** block will be executed. It means both numbers are equal, so we display "*Both numbers are equal.*"

Another solution

```
import java.util.Scanner;

public class BiggerNumberChecker {
    public static void main(String[] args) {
        // Create a Scanner object to read input from the user
        Scanner scanner = new Scanner(System.in);

        // Prompt the user to enter the first number
        System.out.print("Enter the first number: ");
        double number1 = scanner.nextDouble();

        // Prompt the user to enter the second number
        System.out.print("Enter the second number: ");
        double number2 = scanner.nextDouble();
```

```java
        // Determine the bigger number using the Math.max() method
        double biggerNumber = Math.max(number1, number2);

        // Display the result
        System.out.println("The bigger number is: " + biggerNumber);

        // Close the Scanner
        scanner.close();
    }
}
```

In this solution, we use the **Math.max()** method to determine the bigger number between **number1** and **number2**. This method returns the larger of the two arguments. Finally, we display the bigger number to the user.

18. Write a program that asks the user for three numbers and displays the largest one.

```java
import java.util.Scanner;

public class LargestNumberFinder {
    public static void main(String[] args) {
        // Create a Scanner object to read input from the user
        Scanner scanner = new Scanner(System.in);

        // Prompt the user to enter the three numbers
        System.out.print("Enter the first number: ");
        double number1 = scanner.nextDouble();

        System.out.print("Enter the second number: ");
        double number2 = scanner.nextDouble();

        System.out.print("Enter the third number: ");
        double number3 = scanner.nextDouble();

        // Find the largest number using if statements
        double largestNumber;

        if (number1 >= number2 && number1 >= number3) {
            largestNumber = number1;
        } else if (number2 >= number1 && number2 >= number3) {
            largestNumber = number2;
        } else {
```

```
            largestNumber = number3;
        }

        // Display the largest number
        System.out.println("The largest number is: " +
 largestNumber);

        // Close the Scanner
        scanner.close();
    }
}
```

We start by importing the ***java.util.Scanner*** class, which allows us to read user input from the console. This class is part of the Java standard library and makes it easy to handle user input.

Next, we define the ***LargestNumberFinder*** class, which will contain our main method.

Inside the ***main*** method, we create a ***Scanner*** object named ***scanner*** to read input from the user. We use this object to obtain the user's input for three numbers.

We prompt the user to enter the three numbers using ***System.out.print*** and ***scanner.nextDouble()***. The entered values are then stored in variables ***number1***, ***number2***, and ***number3***, respectively.

We use ***if*** statements to compare the three numbers and determine the largest one. Here's how the ***if*** statements work:

- The first ***if*** statement checks if ***number1*** is greater than or equal to both ***number2*** and ***number3***. If this condition is ***true***, it means that ***number1*** is the largest number among the three, so we assign its value to the variable ***largestNumber***.
- The first ***else if*** statement checks if ***number2*** is greater than or equal to both ***number1*** and ***number3***. If this condition is ***true***, it means that ***number2*** is the largest number among the three, so we assign its value to the variable ***largestNumber***.
- If neither of the above conditions is ***true***, it means that ***number3*** is the largest number among the three, so we assign its value to the variable ***largestNumber***.

Finally, we use ***System.out.println*** to display the largest number to the user.

We close the ***Scanner*** object to free up system resources using the ***scanner.close()*** method. This step is essential to prevent resource leaks and should be done when we are done using the ***Scanner***.

Another solution

```
import java.util.Scanner;
```

```java
public class LargestNumberFinder {
    public static void main(String[] args) {
        // Create a Scanner object to read input from the user
        Scanner scanner = new Scanner(System.in);

        // Prompt the user to enter the three numbers
        System.out.print("Enter the first number: ");
        double number1 = scanner.nextDouble();

        System.out.print("Enter the second number: ");
        double number2 = scanner.nextDouble();

        System.out.print("Enter the third number: ");
        double number3 = scanner.nextDouble();

        // Find the largest number using the Math.max() method
        double largestNumber = Math.max(number1, Math.max(number2,
number3));

        // Display the largest number
        System.out.println("The largest number is: " +
largestNumber);

        // Close the Scanner
        scanner.close();
    }
}
```

In this program, we prompt the user to enter three numbers. The entered values are then stored in variables *number1*, *number2*, and *number3*, respectively. We use nested *Math.max()* method calls to find the largest number among the three. The *Math.max()* method returns the larger of the two arguments provided to it, so by nesting three calls, we can find the largest number among the three

19. Write a program that reads a number and reports whether it is odd or even.

```java
import java.util.Scanner;

public class OddEvenChecker {
    public static void main(String[] args) {
        // Create a Scanner object to read input from the user
        Scanner scanner = new Scanner(System.in);
```

```java
        // Prompt the user to enter a number
        System.out.print("Enter a number: ");
        int number = scanner.nextInt();

        // Check if the number is odd or even using the modulo
operator (%)
        if (number % 2 == 0) {
            System.out.println(number + " is even.");
        } else {
            System.out.println(number + " is odd.");
        }

        // Close the Scanner
        scanner.close();
    }
}
```

In this program, we prompt the user to enter a number using **System.out.print** and **scanner.nextInt()**. The entered value is then stored in the variable **number**.

We use the modulo operator **%** to check if the number is odd or even. When a number is divided by 2, the remainder will be 0 if it's even and 1 if it's odd. So, if **number % 2 == 0**, it means the number is even, and we display "*is even.*" Otherwise, if **number % 2 != 0**, it means the number is odd, and we display "*is odd.*"

20. Write a program that reads a number and reports whether it is positive, negative or zero.

```java
import java.util.Scanner;

public class NumberClassifier {
    public static void main(String[] args) {
        // Create a Scanner object to read input from the user
        Scanner scanner = new Scanner(System.in);

        // Prompt the user to enter a number
        System.out.print("Enter a number: ");
        double number = scanner.nextDouble();

        // Check if the number is positive, negative, or zero using
if-else statements
        if (number > 0) {
```

```java
            System.out.println("The number is positive.");
        } else if (number < 0) {
            System.out.println("The number is negative.");
        } else {
            System.out.println("The number is zero.");
        }

        // Close the Scanner
        scanner.close();
    }
}
```

In this program, we prompt the user to enter a number using **System.out.print** and **scanner.nextDouble()**. The entered value is then stored in the variable **number**.

We use **if-else** statements to check if the number is positive, negative, or zero:

-   If **number** is greater than 0 (**number > 0**), it means the number is positive, and we display "*The number is positive.*"
-   If **number** is less than 0 (**number < 0**), it means the number is negative, and we display "*The number is negative.*"
-   If neither of the above conditions is **true**, it means **number** is equal to 0, and we display "*The number is zero.*"

21. Make a program that reads the scores of two tests and reports whether the student passed (score greater than or equal to 6) or failed (score less than 6) in each of the tests.

```java
import java.util.Scanner;

public class TestResults {
    public static void main(String[] args) {
        // Create a Scanner object to read input from the user
        Scanner scanner = new Scanner(System.in);

        // Prompt the user to enter the score of the first test
        System.out.print("Enter the score of the first test: ");
        double test1Score = scanner.nextDouble();

        // Prompt the user to enter the score of the second test
        System.out.print("Enter the score of the second test: ");
        double test2Score = scanner.nextDouble();

        // Check if the student passed or failed in the first test
```

```java
        if (test1Score >= 6) {
            System.out.println("You passed the first test.");
        } else {
            System.out.println("You failed the first test.");
        }

        // Check if the student passed or failed in the second test
        if (test2Score >= 6) {
            System.out.println("You passed the second test.");
        } else {
            System.out.println("You failed the second test.");
        }

        // Close the Scanner
        scanner.close();
    }
}
```

We start by importing the ***java.util.Scanner*** class, which allows us to read user input from the console. This class is part of the Java standard library and makes it easy to handle user input.

Next, we define the ***TestResults*** class, which will contain our main method.

Inside the ***main*** method, we create a ***Scanner*** object named ***scanner*** to read input from the user. We use this object to obtain the user's input for the scores of both tests.

We prompt the user to enter the score of the first test using ***System.out.print*** and ***scanner.nextDouble()***. The entered value is then stored in the variable ***test1Score***.

Similarly, we prompt the user to enter the score of the second test using ***System.out.print*** and ***scanner.nextDouble()***. The entered value is then stored in the variable ***test2Score***.

We use ***if*** statements to check if the student passed or failed in each of the tests.

- If the ***test1Score*** is greater than or equal to 6, it means the student passed the first test, so we display "*You passed the first test.*" Otherwise, we display "*You failed the first test.*"
- Similarly, if the ***test2Score*** is greater than or equal to 6, it means the student passed the second test, so we display "*You passed the second test.*" Otherwise, we display "*You failed the second test.*"

22. Make a program that reads the grades of two tests, calculates the simple arithmetic mean, and informs whether the student passed (average greater than or equal to 6) or failed (average less than 6).

```java
import java.util.Scanner;

public class TestGradesChecker {
    public static void main(String[] args) {
        // Create a Scanner object to read input from the user
        Scanner scanner = new Scanner(System.in);

        // Prompt the user to enter the grades of two tests
        System.out.print("Enter the grade of the first test: ");
        double grade1 = scanner.nextDouble();

        System.out.print("Enter the grade of the second test: ");
        double grade2 = scanner.nextDouble();

        // Calculate the average grade
        double average = (grade1 + grade2) / 2;

        // Determine if the student passed or failed based on the average
        if (average >= 6) {
            System.out.println("Congratulations! You passed.");
        } else {
            System.out.println("Sorry, you failed.");
        }

        // Close the Scanner
        scanner.close();
    }
}
```

We start by importing the ***java.util.Scanner*** class, which allows us to read user input from the console. This class is part of the Java standard library and makes it easy to handle user input.

Next, we define the ***TestGradesChecker*** class, which will contain our main method.

Inside the ***main*** method, we create a ***Scanner*** object named ***scanner*** to read input from the user. We use this object to obtain the user's input for the grades of the two tests.

We prompt the user to enter the grade of the first test using **System.out.print** and **scanner.nextDouble()**. The entered value is then stored in the variable **grade1**.

Similarly, we prompt the user to enter the grade of the second test using **System.out.print** and **scanner.nextDouble()**. The entered value is then stored in the variable **grade2**.

We calculate the average grade by adding the grades of the two tests and dividing the sum by 2.

We use an **if** statement to determine if the student passed or failed based on the average. If the average is greater than or equal to 6, it means the student passed, and we display "*Congratulations! You passed.*" Otherwise, if the average is less than 6, it means the student failed, and we display "*Sorry, you failed.*"

We close the **Scanner** object to free up system resources using the **scanner.close()** method. This step is essential to prevent resource leaks and should be done when we are done using the **Scanner**.

23. Make a program that reads three numbers, and informs if their sum is divisible by 5 or not.

```java
import java.util.Scanner;

public class SumDivisibleByFiveChecker {
    public static void main(String[] args) {
        // Create a Scanner object to read input from the user
        Scanner scanner = new Scanner(System.in);

        // Prompt the user to enter three numbers
        System.out.print("Enter the first number: ");
        int number1 = scanner.nextInt();

        System.out.print("Enter the second number: ");
        int number2 = scanner.nextInt();

        System.out.print("Enter the third number: ");
        int number3 = scanner.nextInt();

        // Calculate the sum of the three numbers
        int sum = number1 + number2 + number3;

        // Check if the sum is divisible by 5 and display the result
        if (sum % 5 == 0) {
            System.out.println("The sum is divisible by 5.");
        } else {
```

```
        System.out.println("The sum is not divisible by 5.");
    }

    // Close the Scanner
    scanner.close();
    }
}
```

We prompt the user to enter three numbers using **System.out.print** and **scanner.nextInt()**. The entered values are then stored in variables **number1**, **number2**, and **number3**, respectively.

We calculate the sum of the three numbers using the + operator.

We use an **if** statement to check if the sum of the three numbers is divisible by 5. If the sum is divisible by 5, it means the **sum % 5 == 0**.

24. Create a program that reads three numbers and checks if their sum is positive, negative or equal to zero

```
import java.util.Scanner;

public class SumSignChecker {
    public static void main(String[] args) {
        // Create a Scanner object to read input from the user
        Scanner scanner = new Scanner(System.in);

        // Prompt the user to enter three numbers
        System.out.print("Enter the first number: ");
        int number1 = scanner.nextInt();

        System.out.print("Enter the second number: ");
        int number2 = scanner.nextInt();

        System.out.print("Enter the third number: ");
        int number3 = scanner.nextInt();

        // Calculate the sum of the three numbers
        int sum = number1 + number2 + number3;

        // Check if the sum is positive, negative, or equal to zero
        if (sum > 0) {
            System.out.println("The sum is positive.");
        } else if (sum < 0) {
            System.out.println("The sum is negative.");
        } else {
```

```java
        System.out.println("The sum is equal to zero.");
    }

    // Close the Scanner
    scanner.close();
    }
}
```

We prompt the user to enter three numbers using **System.out.print** and **scanner.nextInt()**. The entered values are then stored in variables **number1**, **number2**, and **number3**, respectively.

We calculate the sum of the three numbers using the + operator.

We use **if** statements to check if the sum of the three numbers is positive, negative, or equal to zero.

- **if (sum > 0)**: This line checks if the variable sum is greater than 0. If the condition is true, it means that the sum of the three numbers is positive.
- **else if (sum < 0)**: If the first condition is false, the else if statement checks if the variable sum is less than 0. If this condition is true, it means that the sum of the three numbers is negative.
- **else**: If both the above conditions are false, it means that the variable sum is equal to 0. In this case, the else block will be executed, and it means that the sum of the three numbers is equal to zero.

25. Make a program that reads three numbers, and displays them on the screen in ascending order.

```java
import java.util.Scanner;

public class AscendingOrder {
    public static void main(String[] args) {
        // Create a Scanner object to read input from the user
        Scanner scanner = new Scanner(System.in);

        // Prompt the user to enter three numbers
        System.out.print("Enter the first number: ");
        int number1 = scanner.nextInt();

        System.out.print("Enter the second number: ");
        int number2 = scanner.nextInt();

        System.out.print("Enter the third number: ");
        int number3 = scanner.nextInt();
```

```java
        // Display the numbers in ascending order
        if (number1 <= number2 && number1 <= number3) {
            System.out.print(number1 + " ");
            if (number2 <= number3) {
                System.out.println(number2 + " " + number3);
            } else {
                System.out.println(number3 + " " + number2);
            }
        } else if (number2 <= number1 && number2 <= number3) {
            System.out.print(number2 + " ");
            if (number1 <= number3) {
                System.out.println(number1 + " " + number3);
            } else {
                System.out.println(number3 + " " + number1);
            }
        } else {
            System.out.print(number3 + " ");
            if (number1 <= number2) {
                System.out.println(number1 + " " + number2);
            } else {
                System.out.println(number2 + " " + number1);
            }
        }

        // Close the Scanner
        scanner.close();
    }
}
```

We use *if* statements to determine the smallest number among the three entered numbers. We compare the three numbers to find the smallest one.

We start by checking if *number1* is the smallest using the condition *number1 <= number2 && number1 <= number3*. If this condition is true, it means that *number1* is the smallest number.

If *number1* is not the smallest, we check if *number2* is the smallest using the condition *number2 <= number1 && number2 <= number3*. If this condition is true, it means that *number2* is the smallest number.

If neither *number1* nor *number2* is the smallest, it means that *number3* is the smallest number.

We then print the numbers in ascending order based on their relationship with the smallest number.

If *number1* is the smallest, we print it first, then we check if *number2* is smaller than *number3*, and print *number2* followed by *number3*.

If *number2* is the smallest, we print it first, then we check if *number1* is smaller than *number3*, and print *number1* followed by *number3*.

If *number3* is the smallest, we print it first, then we check if *number1* is smaller than *number2*, and print *number1* followed by *number2*.

26. Make a program that reads the age of three people and how many of them are of legal age (age 18 or older).

```java
import java.util.Scanner;

public class LegalAgeCounter {
    public static void main(String[] args) {
        // Create a Scanner object to read input from the user
        Scanner scanner = new Scanner(System.in);

        // Prompt the user to enter the age of three people
        System.out.print("Enter the age of the first person: ");
        int age1 = scanner.nextInt();

        System.out.print("Enter the age of the second person: ");
        int age2 = scanner.nextInt();

        System.out.print("Enter the age of the third person: ");
        int age3 = scanner.nextInt();

        // Determine how many of them are of legal age
        int legalAgeCount = 0;

        if (age1 >= 18) {
            legalAgeCount++;
        }

        if (age2 >= 18) {
            legalAgeCount++;
        }

        if (age3 >= 18) {
            legalAgeCount++;
        }

        // Display the number of people of legal age
        System.out.println("Number of people of legal age: " +
legalAgeCount);

        // Close the Scanner
```

```
        scanner.close();
    }
}
```

In this program, we prompt the user to enter the age of three people. The entered values are then stored in variables **age1**, **age2**, and **age3**, respectively.

We use **if** statements to check if each person's age is 18 or older. If a person's age is 18 or older, we increment the **legalAgeCount** variable by 1.

Finally, we display the number of people of legal age using **System.out.println**.

27. Write a program that reads three numbers and tells you if they can be the sides of a triangle (the sum of two sides must always be greater than the third side).

```java
import java.util.Scanner;

public class TriangleSidesChecker {
    public static void main(String[] args) {
        // Create a Scanner object to read input from the user
        Scanner scanner = new Scanner(System.in);

        // Prompt the user to enter three numbers
        System.out.print("Enter the first number: ");
        double side1 = scanner.nextDouble();

        System.out.print("Enter the second number: ");
        double side2 = scanner.nextDouble();

        System.out.print("Enter the third number: ");
        double side3 = scanner.nextDouble();

        // Check if the numbers can form a triangle
        if ((side1 + side2 > side3) && (side1 + side3 > side2) && →
(side2 + side3 > side1)) {
            System.out.println("These sides can form a triangle.");
        } else {
            System.out.println("These sides cannot form a
triangle.");
        }

        // Close the Scanner
        scanner.close();
```

```
        }
}
```

In this program, we prompt the user to enter three numbers, which represent the sides of a triangle. The entered values are then stored in variables *side1*, *side2*, and *side3*, respectively.

We use an if statement in the main method to check if the sides can form a triangle based on the condition that the sum of any two sides must be greater than the third side. The condition to check if the sides can form a triangle is *(side1 + side2 > side3) && (side1 + side3 > side2) && (side2 + side3 > side1)*.

Finally, we display the result based on whether the sides can form a triangle or not.

28. Make a program that reads the year of birth of a person and informs if he is able to vote (age greater than or equal to 16 years old).

```java
import java.util.Scanner;
import java.time.LocalDate;

public class VotingEligibilityChecker {
    public static void main(String[] args) {
        // Create a Scanner object to read input from the user
        Scanner scanner = new Scanner(System.in);

        // Prompt the user to enter the year of birth
        System.out.print("Enter the year of birth: ");
        int yearOfBirth = scanner.nextInt();

        // Get the current year from the system clock
        int currentYear = LocalDate.now().getYear();

        // Calculate the person's age
        int age = currentYear - yearOfBirth;

        // Check if the person is able to vote (age greater than or
equal to 16)
        if (age >= 16) {
            System.out.println("You are able to vote.");
        } else {
            System.out.println("You are not able to vote yet.");
        }
```

```
            // Close the Scanner
            scanner.close();
    }
}
```

In this program, we prompt the user to enter the year of birth of a person. The entered value is then stored in the variable **yearOfBirth**.

We get the current year from the system clock using **LocalDate.now().getYear()**, and store it in the variable **currentYear**.

We then calculate the person's age by subtracting the **yearOfBirth** from the **currentYear**.

Finally, we use an *if* statement to check if the person is able to vote, which means their age is greater than or equal to 16. If the condition is true, we display "*You are able to vote.*" Otherwise, we display "*You are not able to vote yet.*"

29. Make a program that reads a person's age and informs if he is not able to vote (age less than 16 years old), if he is able to vote but is not obligated (16, 17 years old, or age equal to or greater than 70 years), or if it is obligatory (18 to 69 years old).

*These conditions are in accordance with Brazilian legislation.

```
import java.util.Scanner;
import java.time.LocalDate;

public class VotingEligibilityChecker {
    public static void main(String[] args) {
        // Create a Scanner object to read input from the user
        Scanner scanner = new Scanner(System.in);

        // Prompt the user to enter their age
        System.out.print("Enter your age: ");
        int age = scanner.nextInt();

        // Get the current year from the system clock
        int currentYear = LocalDate.now().getYear();

        // Calculate the year of birth based on the current year and
age
        int yearOfBirth = currentYear - age;

        // Check voting eligibility based on age
        if (age < 16) {
            System.out.println("You are not able to vote.");
```

```
        } else if (age >= 16 && age <= 17) {
            System.out.println("You are able to vote but not
  obligated.");
        } else if (age >= 18 && age <= 69) {
            System.out.println("Voting is obligatory for you.");
        } else {
            System.out.println("You are able to vote but →
  not obligated (age equal to or greater than 70 years).");
        }

        // Close the Scanner
        scanner.close();
    }
}
```

In this program, we prompt the user to enter their age. The entered value is then stored in the variable ***age***.

We get the current year from the system clock using ***LocalDate.now().getYear()***, and we calculate the year of birth based on the current year and the user's age.

Then, we use a series of ***if*** and ***else if*** statements to determine the voting eligibility based on the age conditions specified in the problem.

- If the age is less than 16, the program will display "*You are not able to vote.*"
- If the age is between 16 and 17 (inclusive), the program will display "*You are able to vote but not obligated.*"
- If the age is between 18 and 69 (inclusive), the program will display "*Voting is obligatory for you.*"
- If the age is equal to or greater than 70, the program will display "*You are able to vote but not obligated (age equal to or greater than 70 years).*"

30. Make a program that reads three grades from a student and reports whether he passed (final grade greater than or equal to 7), failed (final grade less than 4) or was in recovery (final grade between 4 and 7).

```
import java.util.Scanner;

public class StudentGradeChecker {
    public static void main(String[] args) {
        // Create a Scanner object to read input from the user
        Scanner scanner = new Scanner(System.in);
```

```java
    // Prompt the user to enter three grades
    System.out.print("Enter the first grade: ");
    double grade1 = scanner.nextDouble();

    System.out.print("Enter the second grade: ");
    double grade2 = scanner.nextDouble();

    System.out.print("Enter the third grade: ");
    double grade3 = scanner.nextDouble();

    // Calculate the average grade
    double average = (grade1 + grade2 + grade3) / 3.0;

    // Check the student's final result based on the average
grade
    if (average >= 7.0) {
        System.out.println("Passed");
    } else if (average < 4.0) {
        System.out.println("Failed");
    } else {
        System.out.println("In recovery");
    }

    // Close the Scanner
    scanner.close();
    }
}
```

We start by prompting the user to enter three grades using the ***input*** function. The ***float*** function is used to convert the input into floating-point numbers.

After obtaining the grades, we calculate the average grade by summing up the three grades and dividing by 3.

We use ***if***, ***elif***, and ***else*** statements to check the final result based on the average grade.

If the average grade is greater than or equal to 7, we set the result as "*Pass*".

If the average grade is less than 4, we set the result as "*Fail*".

For all other average grade values (between 4 and 7), we set the result as "*Recovery*".

We use the *print* function to display the final result to the user.

The program will inform the final result of the student as pass, fail, or in recovery based on the average grade.

31. Write a program that asks for the name of a day of the week and displays whether it is a weekday (Monday to Friday) or a weekend day (Saturday and Sunday).

```java
import java.util.Scanner;

public class DayOfWeekChecker {
    public static void main(String[] args) {
        // Create a Scanner object to read input from the user
        Scanner scanner = new Scanner(System.in);

        // Prompt the user to enter the name of a day
        System.out.print("Enter the name of a day of the week: ");
        String day = scanner.nextLine().toLowerCase();
        // Convert the input to lowercase for case-insensitive
comparison

        // Check if the entered day is a weekday or a weekend day
        if (day.equals("saturday") || day.equals("sunday")) {
            System.out.println("It's a weekend day.");
        } else if (day.equals("monday") || day.equals("tuesday")
                || day.equals("wednesday")
                || day.equals("thursday") || day.equals("friday")) {
            System.out.println("It's a weekday.");
        } else {
            System.out.println("Invalid input. →
Please enter a valid day of the week.");
        }

        // Close the Scanner
        scanner.close();
    }
}
```

In this program, we prompt the user to enter the name of a day of the week. The entered value is then stored in the variable *day*.

We use *toLowerCase()* method on the day string to convert it to lowercase, ensuring case-insensitive comparison for the day names.

Then, we use *if* and *else if* statements to check if the entered day is a weekend day (Saturday or Sunday) or a weekday (Monday to Friday).

- If the entered day is "*saturday*" or "*sunday*", the program will display "*It's a weekend day.*"
- If the entered day is "*monday*", "*tuesday*", "*wednesday*", "*thursday*", or "*friday*", the program will display "*It's a weekday.*"

- If the entered day is not any of the valid day names, the program will display "*Invalid input. Please enter a valid day of the week.*"

32. Write a program that asks for a person's height and weight and calculates their body mass index (BMI), displaying the corresponding category (underweight, normal weight, overweight, obese, severely obese).

```java
import java.util.Scanner;

public class BMICalculator {
    public static void main(String[] args) {
        // Create a Scanner object to read input from the user
        Scanner scanner = new Scanner(System.in);

        // Prompt the user to enter their height and weight
        System.out.print("Enter your height in meters: ");
        double height = scanner.nextDouble();

        System.out.print("Enter your weight in kilograms: ");
        double weight = scanner.nextDouble();

        // Calculate the BMI
        double bmi = weight / (height * height);

        // Display the BMI
        System.out.println("Your BMI is: " + bmi);

        // Determine the BMI category
        if (bmi < 16) {
            System.out.println("Category: Severely underweight");
        } else if (bmi >= 16 && bmi < 17) {
            System.out.println("Category: Underweight");
        } else if (bmi >= 17 && bmi < 18.5) {
            System.out.println("Category: Mildly underweight");
        } else if (bmi >= 18.5 && bmi < 25) {
            System.out.println("Category: Normal weight");
        } else if (bmi >= 25 && bmi < 30) {
            System.out.println("Category: Overweight");
        } else if (bmi >= 30 && bmi < 35) {
            System.out.println("Category: Obese Class I (Moderately obese)");
        } else if (bmi >= 35 && bmi < 40) {
```

```
                System.out.println("Category: Obese Class II (Severely
obese)");
          } else {
                System.out.println("Category: Obese Class III (Very
severely → obese)");
          }

          // Close the Scanner
          scanner.close();
      }
}
```

In this program, we prompt the user to enter their height in meters and weight in kilograms. The entered values are then stored in variables **height** and **weight**, respectively.

We calculate the BMI using the formula **weight / (height * height)** and store it in the variable **bmi**.

Then, we display the calculated BMI to the user.

Next, we use a series of **if** and **else if** statements to determine the BMI category based on the calculated BMI value. The program checks the BMI value against specific ranges to determine the corresponding category.

Finally, the program displays the BMI category to the user based on the calculated BMI value.

33. Write a program that asks for an integer and checks if it is divisible by 3 and 5 at the same time.

```
import java.util.Scanner;

public class DivisibleByThreeAndFiveChecker {
    public static void main(String[] args) {
        // Create a Scanner object to read input from the user
        Scanner scanner = new Scanner(System.in);

        // Prompt the user to enter an integer
        System.out.print("Enter an integer: ");
        int number = scanner.nextInt();

        // Check if the number is divisible by 3 and 5 at the same
time
        if (number % 3 == 0 && number % 5 == 0) {
            System.out.println("The number is divisible by both 3
and 5.");
        } else {
```

```java
        System.out.println("The number is not divisible by both
3 and 5.");
        }

        // Close the Scanner
        scanner.close();
    }
}
```

In this program, we prompt the user to enter an integer. The entered value is then stored in the variable **number**.

We use an if statement to check if the number is divisible by 3 and 5 at the same time. We do this by using the modulo operator **%,** which gives us the remainder of the division. If the remainder is 0 for both divisions (**number % 3 == 0 and number % 5 == 0**), then the number is divisible by both 3 and 5.

If the condition is true, the program will display "*The number is divisible by both 3 and 5.*" Otherwise, it will display "*The number is not divisible by both 3 and 5.*"

34. Create a program that asks for a person's age and displays whether they are a child (0-12 years old), teenager (13-17 years old), adult (18-59 years old), or elderly (60 years old or older).

```java
import java.util.Scanner;

public class AgeCategoryChecker {
    public static void main(String[] args) {
        // Create a Scanner object to read input from the user
        Scanner scanner = new Scanner(System.in);

        // Prompt the user to enter their age
        System.out.print("Enter your age: ");
        int age = scanner.nextInt();

        // Check the age category
        if (age >= 0 && age <= 12) {
            System.out.println("You are a child.");
        } else if (age >= 13 && age <= 17) {
            System.out.println("You are a teenager.");
        } else if (age >= 18 && age <= 59) {
            System.out.println("You are an adult.");
        } else {
            System.out.println("You are elderly.");
        }
```

```
        // Close the Scanner
        scanner.close();
    }
}
```

In this program, we prompt the user to enter their age. The entered value is then stored in the variable **age**.

We use **if** and **else if** statements to check the age category based on the age range specified in the problem:
- If the age is between 0 and 12 (inclusive), the program will display "*You are a child.*"
- If the age is between 13 and 17 (inclusive), the program will display "*You are a teenager.*"
- If the age is between 18 and 59 (inclusive), the program will display "*You are an adult.*"
- If the age is 60 or older, the program will display "*You are elderly.*"

35. Make a program that asks for two numbers and displays if the first is divisible by the second

```java
import java.util.Scanner;

public class DivisibilityChecker {
    public static void main(String[] args) {
        // Create a Scanner object to read input from the user
        Scanner scanner = new Scanner(System.in);

        // Prompt the user to enter the first number
        System.out.print("Enter the first number: ");
        int number1 = scanner.nextInt();

        // Prompt the user to enter the second number
        System.out.print("Enter the second number: ");
        int number2 = scanner.nextInt();

        // Check if the first number is divisible by the second
number
        if (number2 != 0 && number1 % number2 == 0) {
            System.out.println(number1 + " is divisible by " +
number2);
        } else {
            System.out.println(number1 + " is not divisible by " +
number2);
```

```
        }

        // Close the Scanner
        scanner.close();
    }
}
```

In this program, we prompt the user to enter the first number and the second number. The entered values are then stored in variables **number1** and **number2**, respectively.

We use an **if** statement to check if the second number is not zero (to avoid division by zero) and if the first number is divisible by the second number. We do this by using the modulo operator **%**, which gives us the remainder of the division. If the remainder is zero (**number1 % number2 == 0**), then the first number is divisible by the second number.

If the condition is true, the program will display the message "*number1 is divisible by number2*". Otherwise, it will display the message "*number1 is not divisible by number2*".

Repeat Loops

In Java, there are three main types of loop structures: *for*, *while*, and *do-while*.

For Loop

The *for* loop has the structure *for (initialization; termination; increment)*. It is useful when you know exactly how many times you want to loop through a block of code.

```java
for (int i = 0; i < 5; i++) {
    System.out.println("Count: " + i);
}
```

In this example, $i = 0$ is the initialization, $i < 5$ is the termination condition, and $i++$ is the increment operation done after each loop iteration.

While Loop

The *while* loop repeatedly executes a block of code as long as a particular condition is true.

```java
int i = 0;
while (i < 5) {
    System.out.println("Count: " + i);
    i++;
}
```

In this example, the loop will continue to print and increment i as long as $i < 5$.

Do-While Loop

The *do-while* loop is similar to the *while* loop, except the condition is evaluated at the end of each loop iteration. This means that a *do-while* loop will run the code block at least once.

```java
int i = 0;
do {
    System.out.println("Count: " + i);
    i++;
} while (i < 5);
```

In all these loop types, you can use **break** to exit the loop early, and **continue** to skip the current iteration and move on to the next one.

36. Write a program that displays the numbers 1 through 10 using a loop.

Using *for*

```
public class NumberDisplay {
    public static void main(String[] args) {
        // Use a for loop to iterate from 1 to 10
        for (int i = 1; i <= 10; i++) {
            System.out.println(i);
        }
    }
}
```

We define a public class named ***NumberDisplay***. The class will contain our ***main*** method.

Inside ***the*** main method, we use a ***for*** loop to iterate from 1 to 10. The loop variable *i* is initialized to 1 (***int i = 1***), which is the starting point of the loop. The loop will continue as long as *i* is less than or equal to 10 (*i <= 10*). After each iteration, the loop variable *i* is incremented by 1 (*i++*).

Inside the loop body (enclosed within curly braces), we use ***System.out.println(i)*** to display the value of the loop variable *i* on the console. This line of code will execute 10 times, once for each iteration of the loop, and will display the numbers 1 through 10 one after the other.

The ***for*** loop will continue until the loop variable *i* is no longer less than or equal to 10. Once *i* becomes 11, the loop will terminate, and the program will move on to the next line of code after the loop.

Since there is no more code after the loop, the program will terminate, and the execution will end.

Using *while*

```
public class NumberDisplay {
    public static void main(String[] args) {
        // Initialize the loop variable i to 1
        int i = 1;

        // Use a while loop to iterate from 1 to 10
        while (i <= 10) {
            System.out.println(i);
            // Increment the loop variable i by 1 for the next
iteration
            i++;
        }
    }
}
```

In this program, we use a **while** loop to iterate from 1 to 10. We first initialize the loop variable *i* to 1 (*int i = 1*), which is the starting point of the loop.

The while loop's condition is *i <= 10*, meaning the loop will continue as long as *i* is less than or equal to 10. Inside the loop body (enclosed within curly braces), we use **System.out.println(i)** to display the value of the loop variable *i* on the console.

After displaying the value of *i*, we increment the loop variable *i* by 1 (*i++*) so that it takes the value of the next number in the sequence (2, 3, 4, and so on). The loop will keep running and displaying the numbers until the loop condition *i <= 10* becomes false when *i* becomes 11.

37. Write a program that displays all numbers from 1 to 100

```
public class NumberDisplay {
    public static void main(String[] args) {
        // Use a for loop to iterate from 1 to 100
        for (int i = 1; i <= 100; i++) {
            System.out.println(i);
        }
    }
}
```

In this program, we use a *for* loop to iterate from 1 to 100. The loop variable *i* is initialized to 1 (*int i = 1*), and the loop will continue as long as *i* is less than or equal to 100 (*i <= 100*). After each iteration, the loop variable *i* is incremented by 1 (*i++*).

Inside the loop body, we use **System.out.println(i)** to display the value of *i* on the console. The loop will run 100 times, and all numbers from 1 to 100 will be displayed one after the other.

38. Write a program that prints all even numbers from 1 to 100.

Solution 1

```
public class EvenNumberDisplay {
    public static void main(String[] args) {
        // Use a for loop to iterate from 1 to 100
        for (int i = 1; i <= 100; i++) {
            // Check if the number is even
            // (i.e., divisible by 2 with no remainder)
            if (i % 2 == 0) {
                System.out.println(i);
            }
```

```
        }
      }
    }
```

We define a public class named *EvenNumberDisplay*. The class will contain our main method.

Inside the *main* method, we use a *for* loop to iterate from 1 to 100. The loop variable *i* is initialized to 1 (*int i = 1*), which is the starting point of the loop.

The for loop's condition is *i <= 100*, meaning the loop will continue as long as *i* is less than or equal to 100. After each iteration, the loop variable *i* is incremented by 1 (*i++*).

Inside the loop body (enclosed within curly braces), we use an *if* statement to check if the current value of *i* is even. We do this by using the modulo operator *%*, which gives us the remainder of the division. If *i % 2* equals 0, it means that *i* is divisible by 2 with no remainder, and thus, it is an even number.

If the condition is true (i.e., i is even), we use *System.out.println(i)* to print the value of *i* on the console. This line of code will be executed only for even numbers, effectively printing all even numbers from 1 to 100.

The loop will continue iterating until the loop variable *i* becomes 101, at which point the loop condition *i <= 100* will become false, and the loop will terminate.

Since there is no more code after the loop, the program will terminate, and the execution will end.

Solution 2

```
public class EvenNumberDisplay {
    public static void main(String[] args) {
        // Initialize the loop variable i to 2 (the first even
number)
        int i = 2;

        // Use a while loop to iterate and print
        // even numbers from 1 to 100
        while (i <= 100) {
            System.out.println(i);
            // Increment the loop variable i by 2
            // for the next even number
            i += 2;
        }
    }
}
```

In this program, we use a ***while*** loop to print all even numbers from 1 to 100. We first initialize the loop variable ***i*** to 2 (***int i = 2***), which is the first even number in the given range.

The ***while*** loop's condition is ***i <= 100***, meaning the loop will continue as long as ***i*** is less than or equal to 100. Inside the loop body (enclosed within curly braces), we use ***System.out.println(i)*** to print the value of ***i*** on the console.

After printing the current value of ***i***, we increment the loop variable ***i*** by 2 (***i += 2***). This step ensures that we move to the next even number for the next iteration. Since we are incrementing ***i*** by 2, the loop will only print even numbers.

The loop will keep running and printing even numbers until the loop condition ***i <= 100*** becomes false when ***i*** becomes 102.

39. Write a program that displays even numbers 1 to 50 and odd numbers 51 to 100 using a repeating loop.

```
public class NumberDisplay {
    public static void main(String[] args) {
        // Use a for loop to iterate and print even numbers from 1
to 50
        for (int i = 1; i <= 50; i++) {
            if (i % 2 == 0) {
                System.out.println(i);
            }
        }

        // Use a for loop to iterate and print odd numbers from 51
to 100
        for (int i = 51; i <= 100; i++) {
            if (i % 2 != 0) {
                System.out.println(i);
            }
        }
    }
}
```

The first ***for*** loop initializes the loop variable ***i*** to 1 (***int i = 1***), and the loop will continue as long as ***i*** is less than or equal to 50 (***i <= 50***). After each iteration, the loop variable ***i*** is incremented by 1 (***i++***).

Inside the first loop's body, we use an ***if*** statement to check if the current value of ***i*** is even. We do this by using the modulo operator ***%***, which gives us the remainder of the division. If ***i % 2*** equals 0, it means that ***i*** is divisible by 2 with no remainder, and thus, it is an even number.

If the condition is true (i.e., i is even), we use **System.out.println(i)** to print the value of **i** on the console. This line of code will be executed only for even numbers in the range 1 to 50.

The second for loop initializes the loop variable **i** to 51 (***int i = 51***), and the loop will continue as long as **i** is less than or equal to 100 (***i <= 100***). After each iteration, the loop variable **i** is incremented by 1 (***i++***).

Inside the second loop's body, we use an ***if*** statement to check if the current value of **i** is odd. We do this by using the modulo operator **%**. If **i % 2** is not equal to 0, it means that **i** is not divisible by 2 with no remainder, and thus, it is an odd number.

If the condition is true (i.e., i is odd), we use **System.out.println(i)** to print the value of **i** on the console. This line of code will be executed only for odd numbers in the range 51 to 100.

40. Create a program that prompts the user for a number and displays the table of that number using a loop.

```
import java.util.Scanner;

public class MultiplicationTable {
    public static void main(String[] args) {
        // Create a Scanner object to read input from the user
        Scanner scanner = new Scanner(System.in);

        // Prompt the user to enter a number
        System.out.print("Enter a number: ");
        int number = scanner.nextInt();

        // Display the multiplication table using a for loop
        System.out.println("Multiplication Table of " + number +
":");
        for (int i = 1; i <= 10; i++) {
            int result = number * i;
            System.out.println(number + " x " + i + " = " + result);
        }

        // Close the Scanner
        scanner.close();
    }
}
```

In this program, we use a **Scanner** object to read input from the user. We prompt the user to enter a number, and the entered value is stored in the variable **number**.

We then display the multiplication table of the entered number using a *for* loop. The loop variable *i* is initialized to 1 (*int i = 1*), and the loop will continue as long as *i* is less than or equal to 10 (*i <= 10*). After each iteration, the loop variable *i* is incremented by 1 (*i++*).

Inside the loop body, we calculate the multiplication of number and *i* and store it in the variable **result**. We then use **System.out.println** to display the multiplication table entry, showing the number, multiplier (*i*), and the result of the multiplication.

The loop will run 10 times, displaying the multiplication table of the entered number from 1 to 10.

Using *while*

```java
import java.util.Scanner;

public class MultiplicationTableWhileLoop {
    public static void main(String[] args) {
        // Create a Scanner object to read input from the user
        Scanner scanner = new Scanner(System.in);

        // Prompt the user to enter a number
        System.out.print("Enter a number: ");
        int number = scanner.nextInt();

        // Display the multiplication table using a while loop
        System.out.println("Multiplication Table of " + number +
":");
        int i = 1;
        while (i <= 10) {
            int result = number * i;
            System.out.println(number + " x " + i + " = " + result);
            i++;
        }

        // Close the Scanner
        scanner.close();
    }
}
```

In this program, we use a **Scanner** object to read input from the user. We prompt the user to enter a number, and the entered value is stored in the variable **number**.

We then display the multiplication table of the entered number using a *while* loop. We initialize the loop variable *i* to 1 (*int i = 1*). The loop will continue as long as *i* is less than or equal to 10 (*i <= 10*). Inside the loop body (enclosed within curly braces), we calculate the multiplication of number and *i* and store it in the variable **result**. We then use **System.out.println** to display the multiplication table entry, showing the number, multiplier (**i**), and the result of the multiplication.

After each iteration, we increment the loop variable **i** by 1 (**i++**). The loop will run 10 times, displaying the multiplication table of the entered number from 1 to 10.

41. Create a program that displays the table of all numbers from 1 to 10.

```java
public class MultiplicationTable {
    public static void main(String[] args) {
        // Display multiplication table for numbers 1 to 10
        for (int number = 1; number <= 10; number++) {
            System.out.println("Multiplication Table of " + number +
":");
            for (int i = 1; i <= 10; i++) {
                int result = number * i;
                System.out.println(number + " x " + i + " = " +
result);
            }
            System.out.println(); // Add a blank line between tables
        }
    }
}
```

In this program, we use a nested **for** loop to display the multiplication table for each number from 1 to 10. The outer loop iterates over the numbers 1 to 10, and the inner loop calculates the multiplication table for each number.

The outer loop uses the loop variable **number**, which is initialized to **1** (**int number = 1**). The loop will continue as long as **number** is less than or equal to 10 (**number <= 10**). After each iteration, the loop variable **number** is incremented by 1 (**number++**).

Inside the outer loop's body, we print a heading indicating the current number for which we are displaying the multiplication table. Then, the inner loop is used to calculate and print the multiplication table for that number.

The inner loop uses the loop variable **i**, which is initialized to 1 (**int i = 1**). The inner loop will continue as long as **i** is less than or equal to 10 (**i <= 10**). After each iteration of the inner loop, the loop variable **i** is incremented by 1 (**i++**).

Inside the inner loop's body, we calculate the multiplication of **number** and **i** and store it in the variable **result**. Then, we use **System.out.println** to display the multiplication table entry, showing the **number**, multiplier (**i**), and the **result** of the multiplication.

After displaying the multiplication table for the current number, we add a blank line between tables using *System.out.println()*; to make the output more readable.

The outer loop will run 10 times, once for each number from 1 to 10, and will display the multiplication table for each number.

42. Write a program that asks the user for a number N and displays the sum of all numbers from 1 to N.

```java
import java.util.Scanner;

public class SumOfNumbers {
    public static void main(String[] args) {
        // Create a Scanner object to read input from the user
        Scanner scanner = new Scanner(System.in);

        // Prompt the user to enter a number
        System.out.print("Enter a number N: ");
        int N = scanner.nextInt();

        // Calculate the sum of numbers from 1 to N
        int sum = 0;
        for (int i = 1; i <= N; i++) {
            sum += i;
        }

        // Display the sum
        System.out.println("Sum of numbers from 1 to " + N + " is: "
 + sum);

        // Close the Scanner
        scanner.close();
    }
}
```

We begin by importing the *Scanner* class from the *java.util* package. The *Scanner* class allows us to read user input from the console.

We define a public class named *SumOfNumbers*. The class will contain our main method.

Inside the *main* method, we create a *Scanner* object named *scanner* to read user input.

We prompt the user to enter a number *N* using *System.out.print()*, and then we use *scanner.nextInt()* to read the integer input provided by the user. The entered value is stored in the variable *N*.

We declare an integer variable **sum** and initialize it to 0. This variable will be used to accumulate the sum of numbers from 1 to **N**.

We use a **for** loop to calculate the sum of all numbers from 1 to **N**. The loop variable **i** is initialized to 1 (**int i = 1**), and the loop will continue as long as **i** is less than or equal to **N** (**i <= N**). After each iteration, the loop variable **i** is incremented by 1 (**i++**).

Inside the loop body, we add the current value of **i** to the variable **sum**. This means that in each iteration, the value of **i** will be added to the current value of **sum**, effectively accumulating the sum of all numbers from 1 to **N**.

After the for loop, the variable **sum** will hold the total sum of numbers from 1 to **N**.

We use **System.out.println()** to display the sum of numbers from 1 to **N** on the console.

Finally, we close the **Scanner** using **scanner.close()** to release any system resources associated with it.

Using *while*

```java
import java.util.Scanner;

public class SumOfNumbersWhileLoop {
    public static void main(String[] args) {
        // Create a Scanner object to read input from the user
        Scanner scanner = new Scanner(System.in);

        // Prompt the user to enter a number
        System.out.print("Enter a number N: ");
        int N = scanner.nextInt();

        // Calculate the sum of numbers from 1 to N using a while
loop
        int sum = 0;
        int i = 1;
        while (i <= N) {
            sum += i;
            i++;
        }

        // Display the sum
        System.out.println("Sum of numbers from 1 to " + N + " is: "
+ sum);

        // Close the Scanner
        scanner.close();
    }
```

}

We then use a **while** loop to calculate the sum of all numbers from 1 to **N**. We initialize two variables, **sum** and **i**, to 0 and 1, respectively. The **sum** variable will store the total sum of numbers, and the **i** variable will be used as a loop counter.

The while loop's condition is **i <= N**, meaning the loop will continue as long as **i** is less than or equal to **N**. Inside the loop body, we add the current value of **i** to the variable **sum**, and then we increment **i** by 1 (**i++**). This accumulates the sum of all numbers from 1 to **N**.

The loop will run until the loop condition **i <= N** becomes false when **i** becomes greater than **N**.

43. Write a program that calculates and displays the sum of even numbers from 1 to 100 using a repeating loop.

```
public class SumOfEvenNumbers {
    public static void main(String[] args) {
        // Initialize the loop variable i to 1 (the first number to
consider)
        int i = 1;
        // Initialize the variable to store the sum of even numbers
        int sum = 0;

        // Use a while loop to iterate and
        // calculate the sum of even numbers from 1 to 100
        while (i <= 100) {
            // Check if the current number (i) is even
            if (i % 2 == 0) {
                sum += i; // Add the even number to the sum
            }
            i++; // Increment the loop variable for the next
iteration
        }

        // Display the sum of even numbers
        System.out.println("Sum of even numbers from 1 to 100 is: "
+ sum);
    }
}
```

In this program, we use a **while** loop to calculate the sum of even numbers from 1 to 100. We first initialize the loop variable **i** to 1 (**int i = 1**), which is the first number to consider.

We also initialize the variable *sum* to 0 (*int sum = 0*), which will be used to store the sum of even numbers.

The *while* loop's condition is *i <= 100*, meaning the loop will continue as long as *i* is less than or equal to 100. Inside the loop body, we use an *if* statement to check if the current number (*i*) is even.

We do this by using the modulo operator *%*, which gives us the remainder of the division. If *i % 2* equals 0, it means that *i* is divisible by 2 with no remainder, and thus, it is an even number.

If the condition is true (i.e., i is even), we add the value of *i* to the current sum (*sum += i*). This step accumulates the sum of all even numbers encountered during the loop.

After each iteration, we increment the loop variable *i* by 1 (*i++*) to move to the next number for the next iteration.

The loop will keep running and adding the even numbers to the sum until the loop condition *i <= 100* becomes false when *i* becomes 101.

Finally, we display the sum of even numbers from 1 to 100 using *System.out.println()*.

Using *for* loop

```
public class SumOfEvenNumbersForLoop {
    public static void main(String[] args) {
        // Initialize the variable to store the sum of even numbers
        int sum = 0;

        // Use a for loop to iterate and
        // calculate the sum of even numbers from 1 to 100
        for (int i = 1; i <= 100; i++) {
            // Check if the current number (i) is even
            if (i % 2 == 0) {
                sum += i; // Add the even number to the sum
            }
        }

        // Display the sum of even numbers
        System.out.println("Sum of even numbers from 1 to 100 is: "
+ sum);
    }
}
```

The *for* loop initializes the loop variable *i* to 1 (*int i = 1*). The loop will continue as long as *i* is less than or equal to 100 (*i <= 100*). After each iteration, the loop variable *i* is incremented by 1 (*i++*).

Inside the loop body, we use an *if* statement to check if the current number (*i*) is even. We do this by using the modulo operator *%*, which gives us the remainder of the division. If i % 2 equals 0, it means that i is divisible by 2 with no remainder, and thus, it is an even number.

If the condition is true (i.e., i is even), we add the value of i to the current sum (**sum += i**). This step accumulates the sum of all even numbers encountered during the loop.

The loop will run for all numbers from 1 to 100, and it will add the even numbers to the sum.

44. Write a program that calculates and displays the value of the power of a number entered by the user raised to an exponent also entered by the user, using repetition loops.

```java
import java.util.Scanner;

public class PowerCalculator {
    public static void main(String[] args) {
        // Create a Scanner object to read input from the user
        Scanner scanner = new Scanner(System.in);

        // Prompt the user to enter the base number and the exponent
        System.out.print("Enter the base number: ");
        double base = scanner.nextDouble();

        System.out.print("Enter the exponent: ");
        int exponent = scanner.nextInt();

        // Calculate the power using a loop
        double result = 1.0;
        for (int i = 1; i <= exponent; i++) {
            result *= base;
        }

        // Display the result
        System.out.println(base + " raised to the power of " +
 exponent + " is: " + result);

        // Close the Scanner
        scanner.close();
    }
}
```

In this program, we use a **Scanner** object to read input from the user. We prompt the user to enter the base number and the exponent, and the entered values are stored in the variables **base** (as a double) and **exponent** (as an int).

We then use a **for** loop to calculate the power of the base raised to the exponent. We initialize the result to 1.0 (**double result = 1.0**) since any number raised to the power of 0 is 1.

The **for** loop initializes the loop variable *i* to 1 (**int i = 1**). The loop will continue as long as *i* is less than or equal to the exponent (*i* <= **exponent**). After each iteration, the loop variable *i* is incremented by 1 (**i++**).

Inside the loop body, we multiply the current value of **result** by the **base**. This step repeatedly multiplies the **result** by the **base exponent** times, effectively calculating the power.

After the loop, the variable **result** will hold the final value of the base raised to the exponent.

Finally, we display the result of the power calculation using **System.out.println()**.

45. Write a program that asks the user for a number N and says whether it is prime or not.

```java
import java.util.Scanner;

public class PrimeNumberChecker {
    public static void main(String[] args) {
        // Create a Scanner object to read input from the user
        Scanner scanner = new Scanner(System.in);

        // Prompt the user to enter a number
        System.out.print("Enter a number N: ");
        int N = scanner.nextInt();

        // Check if the number is prime
        boolean isPrime = true;

        if (N <= 1) {
            isPrime = false;
        } else {
            for (int i = 2; i <= Math.sqrt(N); i++) {
                if (N % i == 0) {
                    isPrime = false;
                    break;
                }
            }
        }

        // Display the result
        if (isPrime) {
```

```
            System.out.println(N + " is a prime number.");
        } else {
            System.out.println(N + " is not a prime number.");
        }

        // Close the Scanner
        scanner.close();
    }
}
```

In this program, we use a ***Scanner*** object to read input from the user. We prompt the user to enter a number ***N***, and the entered value is stored in the variable ***N***.

We use a boolean variable ***isPrime*** to keep track of whether the number is prime or not. We initialize it to ***true***, assuming the number is prime initially.

Next, we have an ***if-else*** block to check whether the number is less than or equal to 1. If it is, we set ***isPrime*** to ***false*** since numbers less than or equal to 1 are not prime.

If the number is greater than 1, we use a ***for*** loop to check for divisors of the number from 2 up to the square root of the number. If a divisor is found (i.e., the number is divisible by a value of i without a remainder), then the number is not prime, and we set ***isPrime*** to ***false***.

We use ***Math.sqrt(N)*** to calculate the square root of the number, as we only need to check divisors up to the square root to determine primality efficiently.

The loop will continue until it either finds a divisor or finishes checking all potential divisors. If it finds a divisor, it breaks out of the loop to avoid unnecessary calculations.

After the loop, we check the value of ***isPrime*** and display whether the entered number is prime or not using ***System.out.println()***.

When you run this Java program, it will prompt you to enter a number ***N***. After you provide the input, it will determine and display whether the number is prime or not on the console.

46. Write a program that prompts the user for a number N and displays all prime numbers less than N.

```
import java.util.Scanner;

public class PrimeNumbersLessThanN {
    public static void main(String[] args) {
        // Create a Scanner object to read input from the user
        Scanner scanner = new Scanner(System.in);

        // Prompt the user to enter a number N
```

```java
System.out.print("Enter a number N: ");
int N = scanner.nextInt();

// Display all prime numbers less than N
System.out.println("Prime numbers less than " + N + ":");
for (int i = 2; i < N; i++) {
    boolean isPrime = true;

    if (i <= 1) {
        isPrime = false;
    } else {
        for (int j = 2; j <= Math.sqrt(i); j++) {
            if (i % j == 0) {
                isPrime = false;
                break;
            }
        }
    }

    if (isPrime) {
        System.out.print(i + " ");
    }
}

// Close the Scanner
scanner.close();
    }
}
```

In this program, we use a ***Scanner*** object to read input from the user. We prompt the user to enter a number N, and the entered value is stored in the variable ***N***.

We then use a ***for*** loop to iterate through all numbers from 2 to ***N*** - 1. We start the loop from 2 since 2 is the smallest prime number.

Inside the loop, we use a boolean variable ***isPrime*** to keep track of whether the current number is prime or not. We initialize it to ***true***, assuming the number is prime initially.

Next, we have an ***if-else*** block to check whether the number is less than or equal to 1. If it is, we set ***isPrime*** to ***false*** since numbers less than or equal to 1 are not prime.

If the number is greater than 1, we use a nested ***for*** loop to check for divisors of the current number from 2 up to the square root of the number. If a divisor is found (i.e., the number is divisible by a value of j without a remainder), then the number is not prime, and we set ***isPrime*** to ***false***.

The nested loop will continue until it either finds a divisor or finishes checking all potential divisors. If it finds a divisor, it breaks out of the loop to avoid unnecessary calculations.

After the nested loop, we check the value of **isPrime**. If it is still **true**, then the current number is prime, and we display it using ***System.out.print(i + "***
").

The outer loop will continue through all numbers from 2 to **N** - 1, and it will display all prime numbers less than **N**.

When you run this Java program, it will prompt you to enter a number **N**. After you provide the input, it will display all prime numbers less than **N** on the console.

47. Create a program that displays the first N prime numbers, where N is informed by the user, using a loop.

```java
import java.util.Scanner;

public class FirstNPrimeNumbers {
    public static void main(String[] args) {
        // Create a Scanner object to read input from the user
        Scanner scanner = new Scanner(System.in);

        // Prompt the user to enter a number N
        System.out.print("Enter the value of N: ");
        int N = scanner.nextInt();

        // Display the first N prime numbers
        System.out.println("The first " + N + " prime numbers
 are:");
        int count = 0;
        int number = 2;

        while (count < N) {
            boolean isPrime = true;
            if (number <= 1) {
                isPrime = false;
            } else {
                for (int i = 2; i <= Math.sqrt(number); i++) {
                    if (number % i == 0) {
                        isPrime = false;
                        break;
                    }
                }
            }
```

```
            if (isPrime) {
                System.out.print(number + " ");
                count++;
            }
            number++;
        }

        // Close the Scanner
        scanner.close();
    }
}
```

In this program, we use a ***Scanner*** object to read input from the user. We prompt the user to enter a number ***N***, and the entered value is stored in the variable ***N***.

We use a ***while*** loop to find and display the first ***N*** prime numbers. The loop will continue until we find ***N*** prime numbers.

Inside the loop, we use a boolean variable ***isPrime*** to keep track of whether the current number (***number***) is prime or not. We initialize it to ***true***, assuming the number is prime initially.

Next, we have an ***if-else*** block to check whether the number is less than or equal to 1. If it is, we set ***isPrime*** to ***false*** since numbers less than or equal to 1 are not prime.

If the number is greater than 1, we use a nested ***for*** loop to check for divisors of the current number from 2 up to the square root of the number. If a divisor is found (i.e., the number is divisible by a value of i without a remainder), then the number is not prime, and we set ***isPrime*** to ***false***.

The nested loop will continue until it either finds a divisor or finishes checking all potential divisors. If it finds a divisor, it breaks out of the loop to avoid unnecessary calculations.

After the nested loop, we check the value of ***isPrime***. If it is still ***true***, then the current number is prime, and we display it using ***System.out.print(number + " ")***. We also increment the ***count*** variable to keep track of how many prime numbers we have found.

The outer loop will continue to increment ***number*** and check for prime numbers until we find ***N*** of them.

When you run this Java program, it will prompt you to enter a number ***N***. After you provide the input, it will display the first ***N*** prime numbers on the console.

48. Create a program that displays the first N first perfect squares, where N is informed by the user, using a loop.

```java
import java.util.Scanner;
```

```java
public class FirstNPerfectSquares {
    public static void main(String[] args) {
        // Create a Scanner object to read input from the user
        Scanner scanner = new Scanner(System.in);

        // Prompt the user to enter a number N
        System.out.print("Enter the value of N: ");
        int N = scanner.nextInt();

        // Display the first N perfect squares
        System.out.println("The first " + N + " perfect squares
are:");
        int count = 0;
        int number = 1;

        while (count < N) {
            int perfectSquare = number * number;
            System.out.print(perfectSquare + " ");
            count++;
            number++;
        }

        // Close the Scanner
        scanner.close();
    }
}
```

In this program, we use a **Scanner** object to read input from the user. We prompt the user to enter a number *N*, and the entered value is stored in the variable *N*.

We use a **while** loop to find and display the first *N* perfect squares. The loop will continue until we find *N* perfect squares.

Inside the loop, we calculate the square of the current number (**number**) by multiplying it by itself (**number * number**). This gives us the perfect square.

We then display the perfect square using **System.out.print(perfectSquare + " ")** and increment the **count** variable to keep track of how many perfect squares we have found.

The loop will continue to increment **number** and display perfect squares until we find N of them.

When you run this Java program, it will prompt you to enter a number *N*. After you provide the input, it will display the first *N* perfect squares on the console.

49. Write a program that prompts the user for two numbers A and B and displays all numbers between A and B.

```java
import java.util.Scanner;

public class NumbersBetweenAandB {
    public static void main(String[] args) {
        // Create a Scanner object to read input from the user
        Scanner scanner = new Scanner(System.in);

        // Prompt the user to enter two numbers A and B
        System.out.print("Enter number A: ");
        int A = scanner.nextInt();

        System.out.print("Enter number B: ");
        int B = scanner.nextInt();

        // Display numbers between A and B
        System.out.println("Numbers between " + A + " and " + B +
":");

        if (A <= B) {
            for (int i = A; i <= B; i++) {
                System.out.print(i + " ");
            }
        } else {
            for (int i = A; i >= B; i--) {
                System.out.print(i + " ");
            }
        }

        // Close the Scanner
        scanner.close();
    }
}
```

In this program, we use a ***Scanner*** object to read input from the user. We prompt the user to enter two numbers *A* and *B*, and the entered values are stored in the variables *A* and *B*, respectively.

We then use an ***if-else*** block to handle two cases: when *A* is less than or equal to *B*, and when *A* is greater than *B*.

If *A* is less than or equal to *B*, we use a ***for*** loop to iterate through all numbers from *A* to *B*, and we display each number using ***System.out.print(i + " ")***.

If *A* is greater than *B*, we use a *for* loop to iterate through all numbers from *A* to *B* in reverse order, and we display each number using *System.out.print(i + " ")*.

The program will display all numbers between *A* and *B*, regardless of whether *A* is smaller or larger than *B*.

When you run this Java program, it will prompt you to enter two numbers *A* and *B*. After you provide the input, it will display all numbers between *A* and *B* on the console.

50. Write a program that reads numbers from the user until a negative number is entered, and prints the sum of the positive numbers.

```java
import java.util.Scanner;

public class SumOfPositiveNumbers {
    public static void main(String[] args) {
        // Create a Scanner object to read input from the user
        Scanner scanner = new Scanner(System.in);

        // Prompt the user to enter numbers and
        // calculate the sum of positive numbers
        int sum = 0;
        int number;

        do {
            System.out.print("Enter a number (or a negative number
to stop): ");
            number = scanner.nextInt();

            if (number > 0) {
                sum += number;
            }
        } while (number >= 0);

        // Display the sum of positive numbers
        System.out.println("The sum of positive numbers is: " +
sum);

        // Close the Scanner
        scanner.close();
    }
}
```

In this program, we use a **Scanner** object to read input from the user. We use a **do-while** loop to repeatedly prompt the user to enter numbers. The loop will continue until a negative number is entered.

Inside the loop, we read the user's input using **scanner.nextInt()** and store it in the variable **number**.

If the **number** is greater than 0 (positive), we add it to the **sum** variable to accumulate the sum of positive numbers.

The loop will continue prompting for numbers until a negative number is entered.

Once the user enters a negative number, the loop stops, and we display the sum of positive numbers using **System.out.println("The sum of positive numbers is: " + sum)**.

When you run this Java program, you can enter numbers one by one. Once you enter a negative number, the program will stop taking input and display the sum of positive numbers entered before the negative number.

51. Write a program that prompts the user for a number and displays the Fibonacci sequence up to the given number using a repeating loop.

```java
import java.util.Scanner;

public class FibonacciSequence {
    public static void main(String[] args) {
        // Create a Scanner object to read input from the user
        Scanner scanner = new Scanner(System.in);

        // Prompt the user to enter a number
        System.out.print("Enter a number: ");
        int number = scanner.nextInt();

        // Display the Fibonacci sequence up to the given number
        int prevNumber = 0;
        int currentNumber = 1;

        System.out.println("Fibonacci sequence up to " + number +
":");
        System.out.print(prevNumber + " ");

        while (currentNumber <= number) {
            System.out.print(currentNumber + " ");
            int nextNumber = prevNumber + currentNumber;
            prevNumber = currentNumber;
            currentNumber = nextNumber;
```

```
        }

        // Close the Scanner
        scanner.close();
    }
}
```

In this program, we use a **Scanner** object to read input from the user. We prompt the user to enter a number, and the entered value is stored in the variable **number**.

We initialize two variables **prevNumber** and **currentNumber** to represent the first two numbers in the Fibonacci sequence. The first number is 0, and the second number is 1.

We then display the first number in the sequence (0) using **System.out.print(prevNumber + " ")**.

Next, we use a **while** loop to generate and display the Fibonacci sequence up to the given number (**number**). The loop will continue until **currentNumber** exceeds the given number.

Inside the loop, we calculate the next number in the sequence (**nextNumber**) by adding the **prevNumber** and **currentNumber**. Then, we update **prevNumber** to be the current number (**currentNumber**) and **currentNumber** to be the next number (**nextNumber**).

We continue this process until the current number (**currentNumber**) exceeds the given number.

When you run this Java program, it will prompt you to enter a number. After you provide the input, it will display the Fibonacci sequence up to the given number on the console.

52. Write a program that reads numbers from the user until zero is entered, and displays the average of the numbers entered.

```java
import java.util.Scanner;

public class AverageOfNumbers {
    public static void main(String[] args) {
        // Create a Scanner object to read input from the user
        Scanner scanner = new Scanner(System.in);

        // Prompt the user to enter numbers and calculate the
average
        int sum = 0;
        int count = 0;

        while (true) {
```

```java
        System.out.print("Enter a number (or 0 to stop): ");
        int number = scanner.nextInt();

        if (number == 0) {
            break; // Exit the loop when zero is entered
        }

        sum += number;
        count++;
    }

    // Calculate the average
    double average = (double) sum / count;

    // Display the average of the numbers entered
    System.out.println("The average of the numbers entered is: "
 + average);

    // Close the Scanner
    scanner.close();
    }
}
```

In this program, we use a **Scanner** object to read input from the user. We use a **while (true)** loop to repeatedly prompt the user to enter numbers. The loop will continue until the user enters 0.

Inside the loop, we read the user's input using **scanner.nextInt()** and store it in the variable **number**.

If the **number** is equal to 0, we **break** out of the loop using the break statement.

If the **number** is not equal to 0, we add it to the **sum** variable to accumulate the sum of the entered numbers, and we increment the **count** variable to keep track of how many numbers have been entered.

After the loop exits (when **0** is entered), we calculate the average by dividing the **sum** by the **count** and storing the result in the variable **average**.

Finally, we display the average of the entered numbers using **System.out.println("The average of the numbers entered is: " + average)**.

53. Write a program that prompts the user for a list of numbers, until the user types the number zero, and displays the largest and smallest numbers in the list.

```java
import java.util.Scanner;
```

```java
public class LargestSmallestNumbers {
    public static void main(String[] args) {
        // Create a Scanner object to read input from the user
        Scanner scanner = new Scanner(System.in);

        // Prompt the user to enter a list of numbers
        // and find the largest and smallest numbers
        int largest = Integer.MIN_VALUE;
        int smallest = Integer.MAX_VALUE;

        while (true) {
            System.out.print("Enter a number (or 0 to stop): ");
            int number = scanner.nextInt();

            if (number == 0) {
                break; // Exit the loop when zero is entered
            }

            if (number > largest) {
                largest = number;
            }

            if (number < smallest) {
                smallest = number;
            }
        }

        // Display the largest and smallest numbers
        System.out.println("The largest number is: " + largest);
        System.out.println("The smallest number is: " + smallest);

        // Close the Scanner
        scanner.close();
    }
}
```

In this program, we use a ***Scanner*** object to read input from the user. We use a ***while (true)*** loop to repeatedly prompt the user to enter numbers. The loop will continue until the user enters 0.

Inside the loop, we read the user's input using ***scanner.nextInt()*** and store it in the variable ***number***.

If the ***number*** is equal to ***0***, we break out of the loop using the ***break*** statement.

If the **number** is not equal to **0**, we compare it with the current largest and smallest numbers. If it is greater than the current **largest**, we update **largest** to the new value. If it is smaller than the current **smallest**, we update **smallest** to the new value.

After the loop exits (when **0** is entered), we have found the largest and smallest numbers in the list.

Finally, we display the largest and smallest numbers using **System.out.println("The largest number is: " + largest)** and **System.out.println("The smallest number is: " + smallest)**.

54. Write a program that prompts the user for a sentence and displays the number of vowels in the sentence.

```java
import java.util.Scanner;

public class CountVowelsInSentence {
    public static void main(String[] args) {
        // Create a Scanner object to read input from the user
        Scanner scanner = new Scanner(System.in);

        // Prompt the user to enter a sentence
        System.out.print("Enter a sentence: ");
        String sentence = scanner.nextLine();

        // Convert the sentence to lowercase to make it
case-insensitive
        sentence = sentence.toLowerCase();

        // Count the number of vowels in the sentence
        int vowelCount = 0;
        for (int i = 0; i < sentence.length(); i++) {
            char ch = sentence.charAt(i);
            if (ch == 'a' || ch == 'e' || ch == 'i' || ch == 'o' ||
ch == 'u') {
                vowelCount++;
            }
        }

        // Display the number of vowels in the sentence
        System.out.println("Number of vowels in the sentence: " +
vowelCount);

        // Close the Scanner
        scanner.close();
```

```
        }
}
```

In this program, we use a **Scanner** object to read input from the user. We prompt the user to enter a sentence, and the entered value is stored in the variable **sentence**.

Since we want to make the counting case-insensitive (consider both uppercase and lowercase vowels), we convert the entire sentence to lowercase using the **toLowerCase()** method.

We then use a **for** loop to iterate through each character in the sentence. Inside the loop, we use an if statement to check if the character is a vowel (**'a'**, **'e'**, **'i'**, **'o'**, or **'u'**).

If the character is a vowel, we increment the **vowelCount** variable to keep track of the number of vowels found.

After the loop finishes, we display the number of vowels in the sentence using **System.out.println("Number of vowels in the sentence: " + vowelCount)**.

55. Write a program that prompts the user for a number and displays its divisors.

```
import java.util.Scanner;

public class DisplayDivisors {
    public static void main(String[] args) {
        // Create a Scanner object to read input from the user
        Scanner scanner = new Scanner(System.in);

        // Prompt the user to enter a number
        System.out.print("Enter a number: ");
        int number = scanner.nextInt();

        // Display the divisors of the number
        System.out.println("Divisors of " + number + ":");
        for (int i = 1; i <= number; i++) {
            if (number % i == 0) {
                System.out.print(i + " ");
            }
        }

        // Close the Scanner
        scanner.close();
    }
}
```

In this program, we use a **Scanner** object to read input from the user. We prompt the user to enter a number, and the entered value is stored in the variable **number**.

We use a **for** loop to iterate through each number from **1** to **number**. Inside the loop, we use the modulus operator (**%**) to check if the current number is a divisor of **number**. If the remainder is **0**, it means the number is a divisor, and we display it using **System.out.print(i + " ")**.

The loop will continue until all numbers from **1** to **number** are checked.

56. Write a program that determines the lowest common multiple (LCM) between two numbers entered by the user.

```java
import java.util.Scanner;

public class LCMCalculator {
    public static void main(String[] args) {
        // Create a Scanner object to read input from the user
        Scanner scanner = new Scanner(System.in);

        // Prompt the user to enter two numbers
        System.out.print("Enter the first number: ");
        int num1 = scanner.nextInt();

        System.out.print("Enter the second number: ");
        int num2 = scanner.nextInt();

        // Calculate the LCM using the GCD (Greatest Common Divisor)
        int gcd = num1;
        while (gcd % num2 != 0) {
            gcd += num1;
        }

        // Calculate the LCM using the formula LCM = |num1 * num2| / GCD
        int lcm = Math.abs(num1 * num2) / gcd;

        // Display the LCM
        System.out.println("The LCM of " + num1 + " and " + num2 + " is: " + lcm);

        // Close the Scanner
        scanner.close();
    }
}
```

In this program, we use a **Scanner** object to read input from the user. We prompt the user to enter two numbers (**num1** and **num2**), and the entered values are stored in the variables **num1** and **num2**, respectively.

We then calculate the Greatest Common Divisor (GCD) of **num1** and **num2** using a while loop. The loop increments the value of **gcd** by **num1** until **gcd** becomes a multiple of **num2**.

Finally, we calculate the LCM using the formula LCM = |num1 * num2| / GCD and display the calculated LCM using **System.out.println**.

When you run this Java program, it will prompt you to enter two numbers. After you provide the input, it will calculate and display the Lowest Common Multiple (LCM) of the two numbers on the console.

57. Write a program that determines the greatest common divisor (GCD) between two numbers entered by the user.

```java
import java.util.Scanner;

public class GCDCalculator {
    public static void main(String[] args) {
        // Create a Scanner object to read input from the user
        Scanner scanner = new Scanner(System.in);

        // Prompt the user to enter two numbers
        System.out.print("Enter the first number: ");
        int num1 = scanner.nextInt();

        System.out.print("Enter the second number: ");
        int num2 = scanner.nextInt();

        // Calculate the GCD using the Euclidean algorithm
        while (num2 != 0) {
            int temp = num2;
            num2 = num1 % num2;
            num1 = temp;
        }

        // Display the GCD
        System.out.println("The GCD is: " + num1);

        // Close the Scanner
        scanner.close();
    }
}
```

In this program, we use a **Scanner** object to read input from the user. We prompt the user to enter two numbers (**num1** and **num2**), and the entered values are stored in the variables **num1** and **num2**, respectively.

We then calculate the Greatest Common Divisor (GCD) of **num1** and **num2** using the Euclidean algorithm. The algorithm works by repeatedly updating **num1** and **num2** using the formula **num1 = num2** and **num2 = num1 % num2** until **num2** becomes zero. The GCD will be the final value of **num1**.

Finally, the program displays the calculated GCD using **System.out.println**.

When you run this Java program, it will prompt you to enter two numbers. After you provide the input, it will calculate and display the Greatest Common Divisor (GCD) of the two numbers on the console.

58. Write a program that calculates the series below up to the tenth element:

$$ e^x = 1 + x + \frac{x^2}{2!} + \frac{x^3}{3!} + \frac{x^4}{4!} + \cdots $$

```
public class ExponentialSeriesCalculator {
    public static void main(String[] args) {
        int n = 10; // Number of elements in the series
        double x = 2.0; // The value of x for which to calculate e^x

        double result = 1.0; // The first element of the series (e^0
= 1)

        System.out.print("Series for e^x: ");

        for (int i = 1; i <= n; i++) {
            double term = 1.0; // Initialize the term to 1.0
            for (int j = 1; j <= i; j++) {
                term *= x / j; // Calculate the current term (x^i /
i!)
            }
            result += term;
            System.out.print(result + " ");
        }

        System.out.println(); // Move to the next line after
printing the series
    }
}
```

In this program, we initialize n as 10, which represents the number of elements we want to calculate in the series. We also initialize x as 2.0, which is the value for which we want to calculate e^x. We could prompt the user the value of x using a Scanner object.

We start with **result** set to 1.0, as $e^0 = 1$. The for loop iterates from 1 to n and calculates each term of the series using a nested loop. The inner loop iterates from 1 to i, and at each iteration, it multiplies the term by x / j, where j represents the factorial value $i!$. This calculates the i-th term as $x^i / i!$. Finally, we add the term to the **result**.

Using a function

```java
public class ExponentialSeriesCalculator {
    public static void main(String[] args) {
        int n = 10; // Number of elements in the series
        double x = 2.0; // The value of x for which to calculate e^x

        double result = 1.0; // The first element of the series (e^0
 = 1)

        System.out.print("Series for e^x: ");

        for (int i = 1; i <= n; i++) {
            double term = Math.pow(x, i) / factorial(i);
            result += term;
            System.out.print(result + " ");
        }

        System.out.println(); // Move to the next line after
 printing the series
    }

    // Method to calculate the factorial of a number
    private static int factorial(int n) {
        if (n == 0) {
            return 1;
        } else {
            return n * factorial(n - 1);
        }
    }
}
```

In this solution, we calculate each term using **Math.pow** function and a method called **factorial** to calculate $i!$. This method is defined after the **main** method.

59. Rewrite the previous exercise code until the difference between the terms is less than 0.001.

```java
public class ExponentialSeriesCalculator {
    public static void main(String[] args) {
        double x = 2.0; // The value of x for which to calculate e^x

        double term = 1.0; // The first element of the series (e^0 = 1)

        double result = 1.0; // Initialize the result to 1.0

        System.out.print("Series for e^x: " + result + " ");

        int n = 1; // Variable to keep track of the current term number

        do {
            term *= x / n; // Calculate the current term (x^n / n!)
            result += term; // Add the current term to the result
            n++;
            System.out.print(result + " ");
        } while (Math.abs(term) >= 0.001);

        System.out.println(); // Move to the next line after printing the series
    }
}
```

In this updated program, we initialize **x** as 2.0, which is the value for which we want to calculate **e^x**.

We start with **term** and **result** set to 1.0, as e^0 = 1. The **do-while** loop iterates as long as the absolute value of the current term (**term**) is greater than or equal to **0.001**. Inside the loop, we calculate the current term as **x^n / n!**, where **x** is the given value, **n** is the current term number, and **n!** represents the factorial of **n**. We then add the current term to the **result**.

The loop will keep calculating the terms and adding them to the **result** until the difference between consecutive terms becomes less than **0.001**. When this condition is met, the loop terminates, and the program displays the series up to that point.

60. Make a program that calculates the value of sine using the Taylor series according to the equation below until the difference between the terms is less than 0.0001.

$$sen(x) = x - \frac{x^3}{3!} + \frac{x^5}{5!} - \frac{x^7}{7!} + \cdots$$

```java
import java.util.Scanner;

public class SineCalculator {
    public static void main(String[] args) {
        Scanner scanner = new Scanner(System.in);

        System.out.print("Enter the angle in radians: ");
        double x = scanner.nextDouble();

        double term = x; // The first term in the series is x
        double result = term; // Initialize the result to the first term

        int n = 1; // Variable to keep track of the current term number

        do {
            term *= -(x * x) / ((2 * n) * (2 * n + 1));
            // Calculate the next term in the series

            result += term; // Add the current term to the result
            n++;
        } while (Math.abs(term) >= 0.0001);

        System.out.println("The sine of " + x + " radians is: " + result);

        scanner.close();
    }
}
```

We create a **Scanner** object named **scanner** to read input from the user.

We prompt the user to enter the angle in radians (**x**) and read the value using the **nextDouble()** method of the **Scanner** class.

We initialize **term** to **x**, as the first term in the Taylor series is **x**. We also initialize **result** to **term**, as it represents the cumulative sum of the series up to the current term. The variable n is used to keep track of the current term number.

We use a **do-while** loop to calculate each term in the Taylor series expansion of sine. The loop continues until the absolute value of the current term (**term**) becomes less than **0.0001**.

Within the loop, we calculate the next term in the series using the formula **-x^2 / (2n * (2n + 1))**, where n is the current term number. We use **Math.abs(term)** to get the absolute value of **term** and check if it is greater than or equal to **0.0001**. If the condition is true, the loop continues.

At each iteration, we update the **result** by adding the current term to it. This way, **result** represents the cumulative sum of the series up to the current term.

After the loop terminates, we print the result, which represents the value of sine for the given angle in radians.

Arrays

In Java, an array is a container object that holds a fixed number of values of a single type. The length of an array is established when the array is created and cannot be changed afterward.

To declare an array, you define the variable type with square brackets, *[]*.

Here is how you declare an array in Java:

```java
int[] myArray; // declares an array of integers
```

After declaring an array, you must create it with the new keyword, which allocates memory for the array.

```java
myArray = new int[10]; // creates an array of integers with a length
of 10
```

You can also combine these two steps into one:

```java
int[] myArray = new int[10]; // declares and creates an array of
integers
```

Once an array is created, you can access its elements by their index (indices are zero-based). You can also modify an element at a given index:

```java
myArray[0] = 50; // sets the first element to 50
int x = myArray[0]; // reads the first element into x
```

You can determine the length of an array (i.e., the number of elements it can hold) using the ***length*** property:

```java
int length = myArray.length; // gets the length of the array
```

Here is an example that creates an array, assigns values to each element, and then prints each element:

```java
int[] myArray = new int[5];

// assign values to each element
for (int i = 0; i < myArray.length; i++) {
  myArray[i] = i * 10;
}

// print each element
for (int i = 0; i < myArray.length; i++) {
  System.out.println("Element at index " + i + ": " + myArray[i]);
}
```

61. Create a program that reads an array of integers and displays the sum of all the elements.

```java
import java.util.Scanner;

public class ArraySumCalculator {
    public static void main(String[] args) {
        Scanner scanner = new Scanner(System.in);

        // Prompt the user to enter the size of the array
        System.out.print("Enter the size of the array: ");
        int size = scanner.nextInt();

        // Create an array of integers with the given size
        int[] array = new int[size];

        // Prompt the user to enter the elements of the array
        System.out.println("Enter " + size + " integers:");

        for (int i = 0; i < size; i++) {
            array[i] = scanner.nextInt();
        }

        // Calculate the sum of all the elements in the array
        int sum = 0;
        for (int num : array) {
            sum += num;
        }

        // Display the sum of all the elements
        System.out.println("The sum of all the elements is: " +
 sum);

        scanner.close();
    }
}
```

We create a **Scanner** object named **scanner** to read input from the user. We then prompt the user to enter the size of the array and read the value using the **nextInt()** method of the **Scanner** class. The entered value represents the number of elements the user wants to store in the array.

We create an integer array **array** with the size specified by the user. The array will store the integers provided by the user. We then prompt the user to enter the elements of the array one by one using a **for** loop. The loop iterates *size* times, and at each iteration, it reads an integer from the user using the *nextInt()* method and stores it in the corresponding index of the array.

We create an integer variable *sum* and initialize it to *0*. This variable will be used to store the sum of all the elements in the array. We then use a *for-each* loop to iterate over each element (*num*) in the array. At each iteration, we add the value of *num* to the *sum*, effectively calculating the sum of all the elements in the array.

Finally, we use *System.out.println()* to display the sum of all the elements in the array.

62. Write a program that reads an array of integers and displays the largest element in the array.

```java
import java.util.Scanner;

public class LargestElementFinder {
    public static void main(String[] args) {
        Scanner scanner = new Scanner(System.in);

        // Prompt the user to enter the size of the array
        System.out.print("Enter the size of the array: ");
        int size = scanner.nextInt();

        // Create an array of integers with the given size
        int[] array = new int[size];

        // Prompt the user to enter the elements of the array
        System.out.println("Enter " + size + " integers:");

        for (int i = 0; i < size; i++) {
            array[i] = scanner.nextInt();
        }

        // Find the largest element in the array
        int largest = array[0]; // Assume the first element as the
largest

        for (int i = 1; i < size; i++) {
            if (array[i] > largest) {
                largest = array[i];
            }
        }

        // Display the largest element in the array
```

```
        System.out.println("The largest element in the array is: " +
largest);

        scanner.close();
    }
}
```

In this program, we use a **Scanner** to read input from the user. We first prompt the user to enter the size of the array and read the value using **nextInt()**. Then, we create an array of integers with the given size.

Next, we prompt the user to enter the elements of the array one by one using a **for** loop. The loop iterates **size** times, and at each iteration, we read an integer from the user and store it in the corresponding index of the array.

After reading all the elements, we find the largest element in the array using another **for** loop. We initialize the variable **largest** to the value of the first element of the array (**array[0]**). Then, we iterate over the array starting from the second element (**i = 1**) and compare each element with the current value of **largest**. If the current element is greater than **largest**, we update the value of **largest** to the value of the current element.

Finally, we display the largest element in the array using **System.out.println()**.

63. Write a program that reads an array of integers and displays the average of the elements.

```
import java.util.Scanner;

public class ArrayAverageCalculator {
    public static void main(String[] args) {
        Scanner scanner = new Scanner(System.in);

        // Prompt the user to enter the size of the array
        System.out.print("Enter the size of the array: ");
        int size = scanner.nextInt();

        // Create an array of integers with the given size
        int[] array = new int[size];

        // Prompt the user to enter the elements of the array
        System.out.println("Enter " + size + " integers:");

        for (int i = 0; i < size; i++) {
            array[i] = scanner.nextInt();
        }
```

```
        // Calculate the sum of all the elements in the array
        int sum = 0;
        for (int num : array) {
            sum += num;
        }

        // Calculate the average of the elements
        double average = (double) sum / size;

        // Display the average of the elements
        System.out.println("The average of the elements is: " +
 average);

        scanner.close();
    }
}
```

In this program, we use a **Scanner** to read input from the user. We first prompt the user to enter the size of the array and read the value using **nextInt()**. Then, we create an array of integers with the given size.

Next, we prompt the user to enter the elements of the array one by one using a **for** loop. The loop iterates **size** times, and at each iteration, we read an integer from the user and store it in the corresponding index of the array.

After reading all the elements, we calculate the sum of all the elements in the array using another **for-each** loop. The loop iterates over each element (**num**) in the array and adds its value to the variable **sum**.

Next, we calculate the average of the elements by dividing the sum by the size of the array. To ensure that the average is a decimal value, we use (**double**) to cast the **sum** to a **double** before performing the division.

Finally, we display the average of the elements using **System.out.println()**.

64. Create a program that reads two vectors of integers of the same size and displays a new vector with the sum of the corresponding elements of the two vectors.

```
import java.util.Scanner;

public class VectorSumCalculator {
    public static void main(String[] args) {
        Scanner scanner = new Scanner(System.in);

        // Prompt the user to enter the size of the vectors
```

```java
        System.out.print("Enter the size of the vectors: ");
        int size = scanner.nextInt();

        // Create arrays to store the two vectors
        int[] vector1 = new int[size];
        int[] vector2 = new int[size];

        // Prompt the user to enter the elements of the first vector
        System.out.println("Enter the elements of the first
vector:");
        for (int i = 0; i < size; i++) {
            vector1[i] = scanner.nextInt();
        }

        // Prompt the user to enter the elements of the second
vector
        System.out.println("Enter the elements of the second
vector:");
        for (int i = 0; i < size; i++) {
            vector2[i] = scanner.nextInt();
        }

        // Calculate the sum of the corresponding
        // elements and store in a new vector
        int[] sumVector = new int[size];
        for (int i = 0; i < size; i++) {
            sumVector[i] = vector1[i] + vector2[i];
        }

        // Display the new vector with the sum of the corresponding
elements
        System.out.println("The new vector with the sum of the
corresponding elements is:");
        for (int i = 0; i < size; i++) {
            System.out.print(sumVector[i] + " ");
        }

        scanner.close();
    }
}
```

In this program, we use a **Scanner** to read input from the user. We first prompt the user to enter the size of the vectors and read the value using

106

nextInt(). Then, we create two arrays, ***vector1*** and ***vector2***, to store the two vectors.

Next, we prompt the user to enter the elements of the first vector using a ***for*** loop. The loop iterates ***size*** times, and at each iteration, we read an integer from the user and store it in the corresponding index of ***vector1***.

Similarly, we prompt the user to enter the elements of the second vector using another ***for*** loop. The loop iterates ***size*** times, and at each iteration, we read an integer from the user and store it in the corresponding index of ***vector2***.

After reading both vectors, we create a new array ***sumVector*** to store the sum of the corresponding elements of ***vector1*** and ***vector2***. We use another ***for*** loop to iterate over the arrays, and at each iteration, we calculate the sum of the elements at the same index and store it in ***sumVector***.

Finally, we display the new vector ***sumVector*** with the sum of the corresponding elements using a ***for*** loop.

65. Write a program that reads an array of integers and checks if they are in ascending order.

```java
import java.util.Scanner;

public class AscendingOrderChecker {
    public static void main(String[] args) {
        Scanner scanner = new Scanner(System.in);

        // Prompt the user to enter the size of the array
        System.out.print("Enter the size of the array: ");
        int size = scanner.nextInt();

        // Create an array of integers with the given size
        int[] array = new int[size];

        // Prompt the user to enter the elements of the array
        System.out.println("Enter " + size + " integers:");

        for (int i = 0; i < size; i++) {
            array[i] = scanner.nextInt();
        }

        // Check if the elements are in ascending order
        boolean ascending = true;
        for (int i = 1; i < size; i++) {
            if (array[i] < array[i - 1]) {
                ascending = false;
```

```
            break;
        }
    }

    // Display the result
    if (ascending) {
        System.out.println("The elements are in ascending
order.");
    } else {
        System.out.println("The elements are not in ascending
order.");
    }

    scanner.close();
    }
}
```

In this program, we use a **Scanner** to read input from the user. We first prompt the user to enter the size of the array and read the value using **nextInt()**. Then, we create an array of integers with the given size.

Next, we prompt the user to enter the elements of the array one by one using a **for** loop. The loop iterates **size** times, and at each iteration, we read an integer from the user and store it in the corresponding index of the array.

After reading all the elements, we use another **for** loop to check if the elements are in ascending order. We initialize a boolean variable **ascending** to **true**, assuming that the elements are initially in ascending order. Then, we compare each element with the previous element in the array. If any element is less than its previous element, we set **ascending** to **false** and break out of the loop, as this indicates that the elements are not in ascending order.

Finally, we display the result based on the value of the **ascending** variable. If **ascending** is **true**, we print that the elements are in ascending order. Otherwise, we print that the elements are not in ascending order.

66. Write a program that reads an array of integers and displays the elements in reverse order.

```
import java.util.Scanner;

public class ReverseArrayElements {
    public static void main(String[] args) {
        Scanner scanner = new Scanner(System.in);

        // Prompt the user to enter the size of the array
        System.out.print("Enter the size of the array: ");
```

```java
        int size = scanner.nextInt();

        // Create an array of integers with the given size
        int[] array = new int[size];

        // Prompt the user to enter the elements of the array
        System.out.println("Enter " + size + " integers:");

        for (int i = 0; i < size; i++) {
            array[i] = scanner.nextInt();
        }

        // Display the elements of the array in reverse order
        System.out.println("The elements of the array in reverse
order are:");

        for (int i = size - 1; i >= 0; i--) {
            System.out.print(array[i] + " ");
        }

        scanner.close();
    }
}
```

In this program, we use a ***Scanner*** to read input from the user. We first prompt the user to enter the size of the array and read the value using ***nextInt()***. Then, we create an array of integers with the given size.

Next, we prompt the user to enter the elements of the array one by one using a ***for*** loop. The loop iterates ***size*** times, and at each iteration, we read an integer from the user and store it in the corresponding index of the array.

After reading all the elements, we use another ***for*** loop to display the elements of the array in reverse order. The loop starts from the last index (***size - 1***) and iterates in reverse order (***i--***). It prints the element at index ***i***, effectively displaying the array elements in reverse.

67. Create a program that reads an array of integers and finds the second largest element in the array.

```java
import java.util.Scanner;

public class SecondLargestElementFinder {
    public static void main(String[] args) {
        Scanner scanner = new Scanner(System.in);
```

```java
        // Prompt the user to enter the size of the array
        System.out.print("Enter the size of the array: ");
        int size = scanner.nextInt();

        // Create an array of integers with the given size
        int[] array = new int[size];

        // Prompt the user to enter the elements of the array
        System.out.println("Enter " + size + " integers:");

        for (int i = 0; i < size; i++) {
            array[i] = scanner.nextInt();
        }

        // Find the second largest element in the array
        int largest = Integer.MIN_VALUE;
        int secondLargest = Integer.MIN_VALUE;

        for (int i = 0; i < size; i++) {
            if (array[i] > largest) {
                secondLargest = largest;
                largest = array[i];
            } else if (array[i] > secondLargest && array[i] !=
largest) {
                secondLargest = array[i];
            }
        }

        // Display the second largest element in the array
        if (secondLargest == Integer.MIN_VALUE) {
            System.out.println("There is no second largest element
in the array.");
        } else {
            System.out.println("The second largest element in the
array is: " + secondLargest);
        }

        scanner.close();
    }
}
```

In this program, we use a **Scanner** to read input from the user. We first prompt the user to enter the size of the array and read the value using **nextInt()**. Then, we create an array of integers with the given size.

Next, we prompt the user to enter the elements of the array one by one using a *for* loop. The loop iterates *size* times, and at each iteration, we read an integer from the user and store it in the corresponding index of the array.

After reading all the elements, we find the second largest element in the array using another *for* loop. We initialize two variables *largest* and *secondLargest* to *Integer.MIN_VALUE*, which is the smallest possible value for an integer. We then iterate over the array and update these variables accordingly. If an element is greater than the current value of *largest*, we set *secondLargest* to the current value of *largest* and update *largest* to the new element. If an element is greater than the current value of secondLargest but not equal to *largest*, we update *secondLargest* to the new element.

Finally, we display the second largest element in the array. If no second largest element is found (i.e., all elements in the array are the same), we inform the user accordingly.

68. Write a program that reads an array of integers and displays how many times a specific number appears in the array.

```java
import java.util.Scanner;

public class NumberFrequencyCounter {
    public static void main(String[] args) {
        Scanner scanner = new Scanner(System.in);

        // Prompt the user to enter the size of the array
        System.out.print("Enter the size of the array: ");
        int size = scanner.nextInt();

        // Create an array of integers with the given size
        int[] array = new int[size];

        // Prompt the user to enter the elements of the array
        System.out.println("Enter " + size + " integers:");

        for (int i = 0; i < size; i++) {
            array[i] = scanner.nextInt();
        }

        // Prompt the user to enter the specific number to search for
        System.out.print("Enter the specific number to search for: ");
        int specificNumber = scanner.nextInt();
```

```java
        // Count the frequency of the specific number in the array
        int frequency = 0;
        for (int i = 0; i < size; i++) {
            if (array[i] == specificNumber) {
                frequency++;
            }
        }

        // Display the frequency of the specific number
        System.out.println("The specific number appears " +
    frequency + " times in the array.");

        scanner.close();
    }
}
```

In this program, we use a ***Scanner*** to read input from the user. We first prompt the user to enter the size of the array and read the value using ***nextInt()***. Then, we create an array of integers with the given size.

Next, we prompt the user to enter the elements of the array one by one using a ***for*** loop. The loop iterates ***size*** times, and at each iteration, we read an integer from the user and store it in the corresponding index of the array.

After reading all the elements, we prompt the user to enter the specific number to search for and read the value using ***nextInt()***.

We then use another ***for*** loop to count the frequency of the specific number in the array. We initialize a variable ***frequency*** to 0 and iterate over the array. If the element at the current index is equal to the specific number, we increment the value of ***frequency***.

Finally, we display the frequency of the specific number in the array using ***System.out.println()***.

69. Write a program that reads two arrays of integers with the same size and displays a new array with the elements resulting from the multiplication of the corresponding elements of the two arrays.

```java
import java.util.Scanner;

public class ArrayMultiplication {
    public static void main(String[] args) {
        Scanner scanner = new Scanner(System.in);

        // Prompt the user to enter the size of the arrays
```

```java
        System.out.print("Enter the size of the arrays: ");
        int size = scanner.nextInt();

        // Create arrays to store the two arrays
        int[] array1 = new int[size];
        int[] array2 = new int[size];

        // Prompt the user to enter the elements of the first array
        System.out.println("Enter the elements of the first
array:");
        for (int i = 0; i < size; i++) {
            array1[i] = scanner.nextInt();
        }

        // Prompt the user to enter the elements of the second array
        System.out.println("Enter the elements of the second
array:");
        for (int i = 0; i < size; i++) {
            array2[i] = scanner.nextInt();
        }

        // Calculate the new array with the multiplication of
corresponding elements
        int[] resultArray = new int[size];
        for (int i = 0; i < size; i++) {
            resultArray[i] = array1[i] * array2[i];
        }

        // Display the new array with the multiplication of
corresponding elements
        System.out.println("The new array with the multiplication of
corresponding elements is:");
        for (int i = 0; i < size; i++) {
            System.out.print(resultArray[i] + " ");
        }

        scanner.close();
    }
}
```

In this program, we use a **_Scanner_** to read input from the user. We first prompt the user to enter the size of the arrays and read the value using **_nextInt()_**. Then, we create two arrays, **_array1_** and **_array2_**, to store the two arrays.

Next, we prompt the user to enter the elements of the first array using a *for* loop. The loop iterates *size* times, and at each iteration, we read an integer from the user and store it in the corresponding index of *array1*.

Similarly, we prompt the user to enter the elements of the second array using another *for* loop. The loop iterates *size* times, and at each iteration, we read an integer from the user and store it in the corresponding index of *array2*.

After reading both arrays, we create a new array *resultArray* to store the result of the multiplication of the corresponding elements. We use another *for* loop to iterate over the arrays, and at each iteration, we calculate the product of the elements at the same index and store it in *resultArray*.

Finally, we display the new array *resultArray* with the multiplication of the corresponding elements using a *for* loop.

70. Create a program that reads an array of integers and checks that all elements are even.

```java
import java.util.Scanner;

public class AllEvenElementsChecker {
    public static void main(String[] args) {
        Scanner scanner = new Scanner(System.in);

        // Prompt the user to enter the size of the array
        System.out.print("Enter the size of the array: ");
        int size = scanner.nextInt();

        // Create an array of integers with the given size
        int[] array = new int[size];

        // Prompt the user to enter the elements of the array
        System.out.println("Enter " + size + " integers:");

        for (int i = 0; i < size; i++) {
            array[i] = scanner.nextInt();
        }

        // Check if all elements in the array are even
        boolean allEven = true;
        for (int i = 0; i < size; i++) {
            if (array[i] % 2 != 0) {
                allEven = false;
                break;
            }
        }
```

```
        }

        // Display the result
        if (allEven) {
            System.out.println("All elements in the array are
even.");
        } else {
            System.out.println("Not all elements in the array are
even.");
        }

        scanner.close();
    }
}
```

In this program, we use a **Scanner** to read input from the user. We first prompt the user to enter the size of the array and read the value using **nextInt()**. Then, we create an array of integers with the given size.

Next, we prompt the user to enter the elements of the array one by one using a **for** loop. The loop iterates **size** times, and at each iteration, we read an integer from the user and store it in the corresponding index of the array.

After reading all the elements, we use another **for** loop to check whether all elements in the array are even. We initialize a boolean variable **allEven** to **true**, assuming that all elements are initially even. Then, we iterate over the array and check if any element is not even (i.e., if it has a remainder when divided by 2). If we find any odd element, we set **allEven** to **false** and break out of the loop.

Finally, we display the result based on the value of the **allEven** variable. If **allEven** is **true**, we print that all elements in the array are even. Otherwise, we print that not all elements in the array are even.

Strings

In Java, **String** is a built-in class used to manipulate character strings that are immutable (constant and cannot be changed once created). The **String** class provides a number of methods to perform operations on strings such as comparison, concatenation, conversion, trimming, replacing, splitting, etc.

Creating Strings

There are two ways to create String objects in Java:

By string literal:

```
String s1 = "Hello";
```

Java uses a concept called "String pool" to efficiently manage memory used by strings. When a string is created using a literal, the JVM checks the string pool. If the string already exists, it returns the reference of the pool string, else it creates a new string in the pool.

By **new** keyword:

```
String s2 = new String("Hello");
```

This will create a new **String** object in non-pool memory and **s2** will refer to it.

String Concatenation

You can use the + (plus) operator to concatenate two strings.

```
String s1 = "Hello ";
String s2 = "World";
String s3 = s1 + s2;
System.out.println(s3); // Prints "Hello World"
```

String Comparison

There are several ways to compare String objects, including the **equals()** method and the **equalsIgnoreCase()** method.

```
String s1 = "Hello";
String s2 = "hello";
boolean isEqual = s1.equals(s2); // false, because equals is
case-sensitive
boolean isEqualIgnoreCase = s1.equalsIgnoreCase(s2); // true,
because equalsIgnoreCase is not case-sensitive
```

String Length

The **length()** method returns the length of a string.

```java
String s = "Hello";
int length = s.length(); // 5
```

Substrings

The **substring()** method returns a new string that is a substring of the original string.

```java
String s = "Hello";
String sub = s.substring(0, 2); // "He"
```

These are just a few examples of operations you can perform with strings in Java. The **String** class actually provides over 50 methods for various operations.

71. Create a program that reads two words and concatenates them, displaying the resulting word.

```java
import java.util.Scanner;

public class WordConcatenation {
    public static void main(String[] args) {
        Scanner scanner = new Scanner(System.in);

        // Prompt the user to enter the first word
        System.out.print("Enter the first word: ");
        String word1 = scanner.next();

        // Prompt the user to enter the second word
        System.out.print("Enter the second word: ");
        String word2 = scanner.next();

        // Concatenate the two words
        String result = word1 + word2;

        // Display the resulting word
        System.out.println("The resulting word is: " + result);

        scanner.close();
    }
}
```

In this program, we use a **Scanner** to read input from the user. We first prompt the user to enter the first word and read it using **next()**. Then, we prompt the user to enter the second word and read it using **next()** as well.

Next, we concatenate the two words using the + operator. Since both **word1** and **word2** are strings, the + operator performs string concatenation, merging the two words into a single string called **result**.

Finally, we display the resulting word using **System.out.println()**.

72. Write a program that takes a word and displays each letter separately.

```java
import java.util.Scanner;

public class DisplayLetters {
    public static void main(String[] args) {
        Scanner scanner = new Scanner(System.in);

        // Prompt the user to enter a word
        System.out.print("Enter a word: ");
        String word = scanner.nextLine();

        // Display each letter separately
        for (int i = 0; i < word.length(); i++) {
            char letter = word.charAt(i);
            System.out.println(letter);
        }

        scanner.close();
    }
}
```

In this program, we use a **Scanner** to read input from the user. We prompt the user to enter a word using **System.out.print()** and then read the input using **scanner.nextLine()**.

Next, we use a **for** loop to iterate through each character of the word. The loop runs from $i = 0$ to $i = word.length()$ - 1, where **word.length()** gives the number of characters in the word. During each iteration, we use the **charAt(i)** method of the **String** class to get the character at index i of the word, and then we print that character using **System.out.println()**.

As a result, the program will display each letter of the entered word on separate lines.

73. Create a program that takes a sentence and replaces all the letters "a" with "e".

Using *Replace*

```
import java.util.Scanner;

public class ReplaceLetters {
    public static void main(String[] args) {
        Scanner scanner = new Scanner(System.in);

        // Prompt the user to enter a sentence
        System.out.print("Enter a sentence: ");
        String sentence = scanner.nextLine();

        // Replace all occurrences of 'a' with 'e'
        String modifiedSentence = sentence.replace('a', 'e');

        // Display the modified sentence
        System.out.println("Modified sentence: " +
modifiedSentence);

        scanner.close();
    }
}
```

In this program, we use a **Scanner** to read input from the user. We prompt the user to enter a sentence using **System.out.print()** and then read the input using **scanner.nextLine()**.

Next, we use the **replace()** method of the **String** class to replace all occurrences of the letter 'a' in the sentence with the letter 'e'. The **replace()** method takes two characters as arguments and returns a new string where all occurrences of the first character are replaced by the second character.

We store the modified sentence in a new variable called **modifiedSentence**.

Finally, we display the modified sentence using **System.out.println()**.

Using *for* loop

```
import java.util.Scanner;

public class ReplaceLettersWithLoop {
    public static void main(String[] args) {
        Scanner scanner = new Scanner(System.in);
```

```
        // Prompt the user to enter a sentence
        System.out.print("Enter a sentence: ");
        String sentence = scanner.nextLine();

        // Convert the sentence to a character array for easy
manipulation
        char[] charArray = sentence.toCharArray();

        // Loop through each character in the array
        for (int i = 0; i < charArray.length; i++) {
            if (charArray[i] == 'a') {
                // Replace 'a' with 'e'
                charArray[i] = 'e';
            }
        }

        // Convert the character array back to a string
        String modifiedSentence = new String(charArray);

        // Display the modified sentence
        System.out.println("Modified sentence: " +
modifiedSentence);

        scanner.close();
    }
}
```

In this program, we first read the input sentence from the user using a *Scanner* as we did in the previous solution.

Next, we convert the input sentence into a character array using *toCharArray()*. A character array allows us to manipulate individual characters in the sentence.

Then, we use a *for* loop to iterate through each character in the character array. If the current character is 'a', we replace it with 'e' by assigning the value 'e' to the corresponding index in the array.

After looping through all the characters and replacing 'a' with 'e', we convert the character array back to a string using the *String* constructor that takes a character array as an argument.

Finally, we display the modified sentence using *System.out.println()*.

74. Write a program that receives a name and checks that it starts with the letter "A".

```
import java.util.Scanner;
```

```java
public class NameChecker {
    public static void main(String[] args) {
        Scanner scanner = new Scanner(System.in);

        // Prompt the user to enter a name
        System.out.print("Enter a name: ");
        String name = scanner.nextLine();

        // Check if the name starts with the letter "A"
        boolean startsWithA = name.toUpperCase().startsWith("A");

        // Display the result
        if (startsWithA) {
            System.out.println("The name starts with the letter
'A'.");
        } else {
            System.out.println("The name does not start with the
letter 'A'.");
        }

        scanner.close();
    }
}
```

In this program, we use a **_Scanner_** to read input from the user. We prompt the user to enter a name using **_System.out.print()_** and then read the input using **_scanner.nextLine()_**.

Next, we use the **_startsWith()_** method of the **_String_** class to check whether the name starts with the letter "A". The **_startsWith()_** method returns **_true_** if the string starts with the specified prefix and **_false_** otherwise. Since the comparison is case-insensitive, we convert the name to uppercase using **_toUpperCase()_** before checking if it starts with "*A*".

We store the result of the comparison in a boolean variable called **_startsWithA_**.

Finally, we display the result using **_System.out.println()_**.

75. Write a program that reads a word and checks if it is a palindrome (if it can be read backwards the same way).

```java
import java.util.Scanner;

public class PalindromeChecker {
    public static void main(String[] args) {
```

122

```java
Scanner scanner = new Scanner(System.in);

// Prompt the user to enter a word
System.out.print("Enter a word: ");
String word = scanner.nextLine();

// Check if the word is a palindrome
boolean isPalindrome = true;

int left = 0;
int right = word.length() - 1;

while (left < right) {
    if (word.charAt(left) != word.charAt(right)) {
        isPalindrome = false;
        break;
    }
    left++;
    right--;
}

// Display the result
if (isPalindrome) {
    System.out.println("The word is a palindrome.");
} else {
    System.out.println("The word is not a palindrome.");
}

scanner.close();
    }
}
```

In this program, we initialize a boolean variable *isPalindrome* to *true*. This variable will be used to keep track of whether the word is a palindrome or not. We initially assume that the word is a palindrome until proven otherwise.

We use two variables, *left* and *right*, to keep track of the leftmost and rightmost positions of the word.

Then, we implement a *while* loop that runs as long as *left* is less than *right*. Inside the loop, we compare the characters at positions *left* and *right* of the word using *word.charAt(left)* and *word.charAt(right)*. If they do not match, we know the word is not a palindrome, so we set *isPalindrome* to *false* and break out of the loop using the *break* statement.

After the loop, we check the value of *isPalindrome*. If it is *true*, we display the message "*The word is a palindrome.*" If it is *false*, we display the message "*The word is not a palindrome.*"

76. Create a program that reads two words and checks if the second word is an anagram of the first.

```java
import java.util.Arrays;
import java.util.Scanner;

public class AnagramChecker {
    public static void main(String[] args) {
        Scanner scanner = new Scanner(System.in);

        // Prompt the user to enter the first word
        System.out.print("Enter the first word: ");
        String word1 = scanner.nextLine();

        // Prompt the user to enter the second word
        System.out.print("Enter the second word: ");
        String word2 = scanner.nextLine();

        // Remove all spaces and convert to lowercase for
case-insensitive comparison
        word1 = word1.replaceAll("\\s", "").toLowerCase();
        word2 = word2.replaceAll("\\s", "").toLowerCase();

        // Convert the strings to character arrays
        char[] charArray1 = word1.toCharArray();
        char[] charArray2 = word2.toCharArray();

        // Sort the character arrays
        Arrays.sort(charArray1);
        Arrays.sort(charArray2);

        // Compare the sorted character arrays
        boolean isAnagram = Arrays.equals(charArray1, charArray2);

        // Display the result
        if (isAnagram) {
            System.out.println("The second word is an anagram of the
first.");
        } else {
            System.out.println("The second word is not an anagram of
the first.");
        }
```

```
        scanner.close();
    }
}
```

In this program, we use a **Scanner** to read input from the user. We prompt the user to enter the first word using **System.out.print()** and then read the input using **scanner.nextLine()**. Similarly, we prompt the user to enter the second word and read the input.

We then remove all spaces from both words and convert them to lowercase using **replaceAll("\\s", "").toLowerCase()**. This step ensures case-insensitive comparison and removes any spaces that might interfere with the anagram check.

Next, we convert the strings to character arrays using **toCharArray()**.

We sort the character arrays using **Arrays.sort()**.

Finally, we use **Arrays.equals()** to compare the sorted character arrays. If they are equal, the words are anagrams, and we set **isAnagram** to **true**. Otherwise, we set it to **false**.

The program then displays the result using **System.out.println()**.

77. Write a program that takes a full name and displays only the first name.

```java
import java.util.Scanner;

public class FirstNameExtractor {
    public static void main(String[] args) {
        Scanner scanner = new Scanner(System.in);

        // Prompt the user to enter the full name
        System.out.print("Enter your full name: ");
        String fullName = scanner.nextLine();

        // Split the full name by spaces
        String[] nameParts = fullName.trim().split("\\s+");

        // Extract the first name (the first part of the split)
        String firstName = nameParts[0];

        // Display the first name
        System.out.println("Your first name is: " + firstName);

        scanner.close();
    }
}
```

In this program, we use a **Scanner** to read input from the user. We prompt the user to enter their full name using **System.out.print()** and then read the input using **scanner.nextLine()**.

We then use the **split("\\s+")** method on the full name to split it into an array of strings. The regular expression "\s+" matches one or more whitespace characters, which allows us to handle cases where the user enters extra spaces between their first name and last name.

The resulting **nameParts** array contains the first name as the first element, and if the user entered a last name, it will be stored in the subsequent elements.

Finally, we extract the first name from the **nameParts** array and display it using **System.out.println()**.

78. Make a program that receives a sentence and displays the amount of blank spaces present in it.

```java
import java.util.Scanner;

public class BlankSpaceCounter {
    public static void main(String[] args) {
        Scanner scanner = new Scanner(System.in);

        // Prompt the user to enter the sentence
        System.out.print("Enter a sentence: ");
        String sentence = scanner.nextLine();

        // Initialize a variable to count the blank spaces
        int count = 0;

        // Iterate through each character in the sentence
        for (char c : sentence.toCharArray()) {
            // Check if the character is a blank space (space or
    tab)
            if (c == ' ' || c == '\t') {
                count++;
            }
        }

        // Display the number of blank spaces
        System.out.println("Number of blank spaces: " + count);

        scanner.close();
    }
}
```

In this program, we use a **Scanner** to read input from the user. We prompt the user to enter a sentence using **System.out.print()** and then read the input using **scanner.nextLine()**.

We initialize a variable **count** to keep track of the number of blank spaces in the sentence. The variable is initially set to 0.

We then use a **for** loop to iterate through each character in the **sentence**. For each character, we check if it is a blank space (either a space or a tab character). If it is, we increment the **count** variable.

Finally, we display the number of blank spaces using **System.out.println()**.

79. Create a program that reads a word and displays the number of vowels present in it.

```java
import java.util.Scanner;

public class VowelCounter {
    public static void main(String[] args) {
        Scanner scanner = new Scanner(System.in);

        // Prompt the user to enter a word
        System.out.print("Enter a word: ");
        String word = scanner.nextLine().toLowerCase();

        // Initialize a variable to count the number of vowels
        int vowelCount = 0;

        // Iterate through each character in the word
        for (char c : word.toCharArray()) {
            // Check if the character is a vowel (a, e, i, o, u)
            if (c == 'a' || c == 'e' || c == 'i' || c == 'o' || c ==
'u') {
                vowelCount++;
            }
        }

        // Display the number of vowels
        System.out.println("Number of vowels: " + vowelCount);

        scanner.close();
    }
}
```

In this program, we use a **Scanner** to read input from the user. We prompt the user to enter a word using **System.out.print()** and then read the input using **scanner.nextLine()**.

We convert the word to lowercase using **toLowerCase()** to handle both uppercase and lowercase vowels consistently.

We initialize a variable **vowelCount** to keep track of the number of vowels in the word. The variable is initially set to 0.

We then use a **for** loop to iterate through each character in the **word**. For each character, we check if it is a vowel (a, e, i, o, u). If it is, we increment the **vowelCount** variable.

Finally, we display the number of vowels using **System.out.println()**.

80. Write a program that takes a full name and displays the last name (last name) first.

```java
import java.util.Scanner;

public class LastNameFirst {
    public static void main(String[] args) {
        Scanner scanner = new Scanner(System.in);

        // Prompt the user to enter the full name
        System.out.print("Enter your full name: ");
        String fullName = scanner.nextLine();

        // Split the full name into first name and last name
        String[] nameParts = fullName.trim().split("\\s+");

        // Extract the last name (the last part of the split)
        String lastName = nameParts[nameParts.length - 1];

        // Display the last name first
        System.out.println("Last name first: " + lastName);

        scanner.close();
    }
}
```

In this program, we use a **Scanner** to read input from the user. We prompt the user to enter their full name using **System.out.print()** and then read the input using **scanner.nextLine()**.

We then use the **split("\\s+")** method on the full name to split it into an array of strings. The regular expression "\s+" matches one or more whitespace characters, which allows us to handle cases where the user enters extra spaces between their first name and last name.

The resulting **nameParts** array contains the first name as the first element, and the last name as the last element (since we extracted it from the last part of the split).

Finally, we extract the last name from the **nameParts** array and display it first using **System.out.println()**.

Matrices

In Java, a two-dimensional (2D) array is an array of arrays. That means it can hold a table of data with rows and columns. You can think of a 2D array as a grid.

Declaration, Creation, and Initialization of 2D Arrays

Just like one-dimensional arrays, 2D arrays also need to be declared and then created. Here's an example of how to declare, create, and initialize a 2D array:

```
int[][] myArray = new int[5][3];  // Declare and create a 2D array
with 5 rows and 3 columns
```

You can also initialize a 2D array at the time of its declaration, like so:

```
int[][] myArray = { {1, 2, 3}, {4, 5, 6}, {7, 8, 9}, {10, 11, 12},
{13, 14, 15} };
```

In this example, *myArray* is a 2D array with 5 rows and 3 columns.

Accessing 2D Array Elements

You can access elements of a 2D array using two indices – one for the row and the other for the column. Here's an example:

```
int[][] myArray = { {1, 2, 3}, {4, 5, 6}, {7, 8, 9} };
int x = myArray[1][2];  // x will be 6 (second row, third column)
```

Modifying 2D Array Elements

You can also modify elements of a 2D array just like you would with a one-dimensional array:

```
int[][] myArray = { {1, 2, 3}, {4, 5, 6}, {7, 8, 9} };
myArray[1][2] = 10;  // now, myArray[1][2] is 10 instead of 6
```

As you can see, 2D arrays can be very useful for storing table-like data or grids where you need to access elements in two dimensions: rows and columns.

81. Write a program that fills a 3x3 matrix with values entered by the user and displays the sum of the main diagonal values.

```
import java.util.Scanner;
```

```java
public class MainDiagonalSum {
    public static void main(String[] args) {
        Scanner scanner = new Scanner(System.in);

        // Create a 3x3 matrix
        int[][] matrix = new int[3][3];

        // Prompt the user to enter values for the matrix
        System.out.println("Enter the values for the 3x3 matrix:");

        // Fill the matrix with user input
        for (int i = 0; i < 3; i++) {
            for (int j = 0; j < 3; j++) {
                System.out.print("Enter value at position (" + (i+1)
+ ", " + (j+1) + "): ");
                matrix[i][j] = scanner.nextInt();
            }
        }

        // Display the matrix
        System.out.println("The 3x3 matrix is:");
        for (int i = 0; i < 3; i++) {
            for (int j = 0; j < 3; j++) {
                System.out.print(matrix[i][j] + " ");
            }
            System.out.println();
        }

        // Calculate and display the sum of the main diagonal values
        int sumMainDiagonal = 0;
        for (int i = 0; i < 3; i++) {
            sumMainDiagonal += matrix[i][i];
        }
        System.out.println("Sum of the main diagonal values: " +
sumMainDiagonal);

        scanner.close();
    }
}
```

In this program, we use a ***Scanner*** to read input from the user. We create a 3x3 matrix using a 2D array ***int[][] matrix = new int[3][3]***.

We then prompt the user to enter values for the matrix using nested loops. The outer loop runs from 0 to 2 (inclusive) for the rows, and the inner loop runs from 0 to 2 (inclusive) for the columns.

After filling the matrix with user input, we display the matrix using nested loops again. This time, we print the values of the matrix in a row-by-row format.

Next, we calculate the sum of the main diagonal values. The main diagonal consists of elements with the same row and column indices (i.e., **matrix[0][0]**, **matrix[1][1]**, and **matrix[2][2]**). We use a loop to iterate over the main diagonal elements and accumulate their values in the variable **sumMainDiagonal**.

Finally, we display the sum of the main diagonal values using **System.out.println()**.

82. Write a program that fills a 4x4 matrix with random values and displays the transposed matrix.

```java
import java.util.Random;

public class TransposeMatrixWithoutMethod {
    public static void main(String[] args) {
        // Create a 4x4 matrix
        int[][] matrix = new int[4][4];

        // Fill the matrix with random values
        Random random = new Random();
        for (int i = 0; i < 4; i++) {
            for (int j = 0; j < 4; j++) {
                matrix[i][j] = random.nextInt(100); // Generates
random numbers between 0 and 99
            }
        }

        // Display the original matrix
        System.out.println("Original 4x4 matrix:");
        for (int i = 0; i < 4; i++) {
            for (int j = 0; j < 4; j++) {
                System.out.print(matrix[i][j] + " ");
            }
            System.out.println();
        }

        // Transpose the matrix
        int[][] transposedMatrix = new int[4][4];
```

```
        for (int i = 0; i < 4; i++) {
            for (int j = 0; j < 4; j++) {
                transposedMatrix[j][i] = matrix[i][j];
            }
        }

        // Display the transposed matrix
        System.out.println("\nTransposed 4x4 matrix:");
        for (int i = 0; i < 4; i++) {
            for (int j = 0; j < 4; j++) {
                System.out.print(transposedMatrix[i][j] + " ");
            }
            System.out.println();
        }

    }
}
```

We create a 2D integer array named ***matrix*** to represent a 4x4 matrix. This array has four rows and four columns.

Then, we use a nested loop to traverse each element in the matrix. The outer loop (***i***) iterates over the rows, and the inner loop (***j***) iterates over the columns. We use the ***nextInt(100)*** method from the ***Random*** class to generate random integers between 0 and 99 (inclusive) and assign them to each element of the matrix.

We use another nested loop to print the elements of the matrix in a row-by-row format. The outer loop (***i***) iterates over the rows, and the inner loop (***j***) iterates over the columns. For each element, we use ***System.out.print()*** to display its value followed by a space. After printing all elements in a row, we use ***System.out.println()*** to move to the next line and print the next row.

After, we create another 2D integer array named ***transposedMatrix*** to store the transposed version of the original matrix. To obtain the transpose, we swap the rows and columns of the original matrix. The outer loop (***i***) iterates over the rows of the original matrix, and the inner loop (***j***) iterates over the columns. We assign the value of the element at (***i, j***) in the original matrix to the element at (***j, i***) in the transposed matrix. This effectively swaps the rows and columns.

Finally, we use a similar nested loop as in step 3 to print the elements of the transposed matrix in a row-by-row format. The outer loop (***i***) iterates over the rows, and the inner loop (***j***) iterates over the columns. For each element, we use ***System.out.print()*** to display its value followed by a space. After printing all elements in a row, we use ***System.out.println()*** to move to the next line and print the next row.

83. Write a program that reads two 2x2 matrices and displays the sum of the two matrices.

```java
import java.util.Scanner;

public class MatrixSum {
    public static void main(String[] args) {
        Scanner scanner = new Scanner(System.in);

        // Create two 2x2 matrices
        int[][] matrix1 = new int[2][2];
        int[][] matrix2 = new int[2][2];

        // Read the elements of the first matrix from the user
        System.out.println("Enter the elements of the first matrix
(2x2):");
        for (int i = 0; i < 2; i++) {
            for (int j = 0; j < 2; j++) {
                matrix1[i][j] = scanner.nextInt();
            }
        }

        // Read the elements of the second matrix from the user
        System.out.println("Enter the elements of the second matrix
(2x2):");
        for (int i = 0; i < 2; i++) {
            for (int j = 0; j < 2; j++) {
                matrix2[i][j] = scanner.nextInt();
            }
        }

        // Calculate the sum of the two matrices
        int[][] sumMatrix = new int[2][2];
        for (int i = 0; i < 2; i++) {
            for (int j = 0; j < 2; j++) {
                sumMatrix[i][j] = matrix1[i][j] + matrix2[i][j];
            }
        }

        // Display the sum of the two matrices
        System.out.println("Sum of the two matrices (2x2):");
        for (int i = 0; i < 2; i++) {
            for (int j = 0; j < 2; j++) {
```

```
                System.out.print(sumMatrix[i][j] + " ");
            }
            System.out.println();
        }

        scanner.close();
    }
}
```

In this program, we use a 2D integer array to represent each 2x2 matrix: ***int[][] matrix1 = new int[2][2];*** and ***int[][] matrix2 = new int[2][2];***.

We use nested loops to read the elements of both matrices from the user and store them in the respective arrays.

Then, we create another 2D integer array named ***sumMatrix*** to store the sum of the two matrices. We use another set of nested loops to calculate the sum of corresponding elements from ***matrix1*** and ***matrix2*** and store them in ***sumMatrix***.

Finally, we display the sum of the two matrices by using nested loops to print the elements of ***sumMatrix*** in a row-by-row format.

84. Write a program that fills a 5x5 matrix with integers and displays the largest value in the matrix and its position.

```java
import java.util.Random;

public class LargestValueInMatrix {
    public static void main(String[] args) {
        // Create a 5x5 matrix
        int[][] matrix = new int[5][5];

        // Fill the matrix with random integers
        Random random = new Random();
        for (int i = 0; i < 5; i++) {
            for (int j = 0; j < 5; j++) {
                matrix[i][j] = random.nextInt(100); // Generates
random integers between 0 and 99
            }
        }

        // Display the matrix
        System.out.println("Matrix:");
        for (int i = 0; i < 5; i++) {
            for (int j = 0; j < 5; j++) {
                System.out.print(matrix[i][j] + "\t");
```

```
        }
        System.out.println();
    }

    // Find the largest value and its position
    int largestValue = matrix[0][0];
    int row = 0;
    int column = 0;
    for (int i = 0; i < 5; i++) {
        for (int j = 0; j < 5; j++) {
            if (matrix[i][j] > largestValue) {
                largestValue = matrix[i][j];
                row = i;
                column = j;
            }
        }
    }

    // Display the largest value and its position
    System.out.println("\nLargest value: " + largestValue);
    System.out.println("Position: Row " + (row + 1) + ", Column
" + (column + 1));
    }
}
```

We create a 2D integer array named ***matrix*** to represent a 5x5 matrix. This array has five rows and five columns.

Then, we use a nested loop to traverse each element in the matrix. The outer loop (***i***) iterates over the rows, and the inner loop (***j***) iterates over the columns. We use the ***nextInt(100)*** method from the ***Random*** class to generate random integers between 0 and 99 (inclusive) and assign them to each element of the matrix.

After, we use another nested loop to print the elements of the matrix in a row-by-row format. The outer loop (***i***) iterates over the rows, and the inner loop (***j***) iterates over the columns. For each element, we use ***System.out.print()*** to display its value followed by a tab (***\t***). After printing all elements in a row, we use ***System.out.println()*** to move to the next line and print the next row.

We initialize variables ***largestValue***, ***row***, and ***column*** to store the largest value in the matrix and its row and column position. We use another set of nested loops to traverse each element of the matrix. If we find an element greater than the current ***largestValue***, we update the ***largestValue*** and store its row and column positions in the ***row*** and ***column*** variables.

Finally, we display the largest value and its position using ***System.out.println()***. The ***row*** and ***column*** variables hold the index of the largest value in the matrix. However, since array indices start from 0 in Java, we add 1 to both *row* and *column* when displaying the position to show a human-readable format (row and column numbers start from 1).

85. Write a program that reads a 3x3 matrix and calculates the average of the values present in the even positions (sum of the even indices) of the matrix.

```java
import java.util.Scanner;

public class MatrixEvenPositionAverage {
    public static void main(String[] args) {
        Scanner scanner = new Scanner(System.in);

        // Create a 3x3 matrix
        int[][] matrix = new int[3][3];

        // Read the elements of the matrix from the user
        System.out.println("Enter the elements of the 3x3 matrix:");
        for (int i = 0; i < 3; i++) {
            for (int j = 0; j < 3; j++) {
                matrix[i][j] = scanner.nextInt();
            }
        }

        // Calculate the sum of the values in even positions (even
indices)
        int sumEvenPositions = 0;
        int countEvenPositions = 0;
        for (int i = 0; i < 3; i++) {
            for (int j = 0; j < 3; j++) {
                if ((i + j) % 2 == 0) {
                    sumEvenPositions += matrix[i][j];
                    countEvenPositions++;
                }
            }
        }

        // Calculate the average of the values in even positions
        double averageEvenPositions = (double) sumEvenPositions /
countEvenPositions;

        // Display the average of the values in even positions
```

```java
        System.out.println("Average of the values in even positions:
" + averageEvenPositions);

        scanner.close();
    }
}
```

In this program, we use a 2D integer array named **matrix** to represent the 3x3 matrix. We use nested loops to read the elements of the matrix from the user and store them in the **matrix** array.

Next, we use another set of nested loops to traverse each element of the matrix and calculate the sum of the values present in even positions (even indices). We check if the sum of the row index (*i*) and the column index (*j*) is even using the condition *(i + j) % 2 == 0*. If the condition is true, it means the element is at an even position, so we add its value to the **sumEvenPositions** and increment the **countEvenPositions** variable.

Then, we calculate the average of the values in even positions by dividing the **sumEvenPositions** by the **countEvenPositions**.

Finally, we display the average of the values in even positions using **System.out.println()**.

86. Write a program that fills a 4x4 matrix with random numbers and displays the sum of the values present in each row and in each column.

```java
import java.util.Random;

public class MatrixRowColumnSum {
    public static void main(String[] args) {
        // Create a 4x4 matrix
        int[][] matrix = new int[4][4];

        // Fill the matrix with random numbers
        Random random = new Random();
        for (int i = 0; i < 4; i++) {
            for (int j = 0; j < 4; j++) {
                matrix[i][j] = random.nextInt(100); // Generates
random integers between 0 and 99
            }
        }

        // Display the matrix
        System.out.println("Matrix:");
```

```java
        printMatrix(matrix);

        // Calculate and display the sum of values in each row
        System.out.println("\nSum of values in each row:");
        for (int i = 0; i < 4; i++) {
            int rowSum = 0;
            for (int j = 0; j < 4; j++) {
                rowSum += matrix[i][j];
            }
            System.out.println("Row " + (i + 1) + ": " + rowSum);
        }

        // Calculate and display the sum of values in each column
        System.out.println("\nSum of values in each column:");
        for (int j = 0; j < 4; j++) {
            int columnSum = 0;
            for (int i = 0; i < 4; i++) {
                columnSum += matrix[i][j];
            }
            System.out.println("Column " + (j + 1) + ": " +
columnSum);
        }
    }

    // Method to print the matrix
    public static void printMatrix(int[][] matrix) {
        for (int i = 0; i < 4; i++) {
            for (int j = 0; j < 4; j++) {
                System.out.print(matrix[i][j] + "\t");
            }
            System.out.println();
        }
    }
}
```

We create a 2D integer array named **matrix** to represent a 4x4 matrix. This array has four rows and four columns.

Then, we use a nested loop to traverse each element in the matrix. The outer loop (*i*) iterates over the rows, and the inner loop (*j*) iterates over the columns. We use the **nextInt(100)** method from the **Random** class to generate random integers between 0 and 99 (inclusive) and assign them to each element of the matrix.

After, we use the **printMatrix()** method to display the elements of the matrix in a row-by-row format. The **printMatrix()** method takes the **matrix** as input and iterates through its elements to print them.

We use another set of nested loops to calculate the sum of the values in each row. The outer loop (*i*) iterates over the rows, and the inner loop (*j*) iterates over the columns. For each row, we initialize the **rowSum** variable to 0, and then we add each element of that row to the **rowSum**. After calculating the sum of the row, we display it along with the row number.

Finally, we use another set of nested loops to calculate the sum of the values in each column. The outer loop (*j*) iterates over the columns, and the inner loop (*i*) iterates over the rows. For each column, we initialize the **columnSum** variable to 0, and then we add each element of that column to the **columnSum**. After calculating the sum of the column, we display it along with the column number.

87. Write a program that reads a 3x3 matrix and calculates the determinant of the matrix.

```
import java.util.Scanner;

public class MatrixDeterminant {
    public static void main(String[] args) {
        Scanner scanner = new Scanner(System.in);

        // Create a 3x3 matrix
        int[][] matrix = new int[3][3];

        // Read the elements of the matrix from the user
        System.out.println("Enter the elements of the 3x3 matrix:");
        for (int i = 0; i < 3; i++) {
            for (int j = 0; j < 3; j++) {
                matrix[i][j] = scanner.nextInt();
            }
        }

        // Calculate the determinant of the matrix
        int determinant = calculateDeterminant(matrix);

        // Display the determinant of the matrix
        System.out.println("Determinant of the matrix is: " +
determinant);

        scanner.close();
    }

    // Method to calculate the determinant of a 3x3 matrix
    public static int calculateDeterminant(int[][] matrix) {
```

```
        int a = matrix[0][0];
        int b = matrix[0][1];
        int c = matrix[0][2];
        int d = matrix[1][0];
        int e = matrix[1][1];
        int f = matrix[1][2];
        int g = matrix[2][0];
        int h = matrix[2][1];
        int i = matrix[2][2];

        int determinant = a * (e * i - f * h) - b * (d * i - f * g)
+ c * (d * h - e * g);
        return determinant;
    }
}
```

To calculate the determinant of a 3x3 matrix, we can use the formula:

$$\det \begin{pmatrix} 1 & 2 & 3 \\ 4 & 5 & 6 \\ 7 & 8 & 9 \end{pmatrix}$$

$$= 1 \cdot \det \begin{pmatrix} 5 & 6 \\ 8 & 9 \end{pmatrix} - 2 \cdot \det \begin{pmatrix} 4 & 6 \\ 7 & 9 \end{pmatrix} + 3 \cdot \det \begin{pmatrix} 4 & 5 \\ 7 & 8 \end{pmatrix}$$

In this program, we use a 2D integer array named **matrix** to represent the 3x3 matrix. We read the elements of the matrix from the user using nested loops.

The determinant of the matrix is calculated using the **calculateDeterminant()** method. This method takes the matrix as input and uses the formula mentioned above to calculate the determinant. The values of a, b, c, d, e, f, g, h, and i are extracted from the matrix, and the determinant is computed using the formula.

Finally, the determinant is displayed to the user using **System.out.println()**.

Using Sarrus rule to calculate determinant

```
import java.util.Scanner;

public class MatrixDeterminantSarrus {
    public static void main(String[] args) {
        Scanner scanner = new Scanner(System.in);
```

```java
// Create a 3x3 matrix
int[][] matrix = new int[3][3];

// Read the elements of the matrix from the user
System.out.println("Enter the elements of the 3x3 matrix:");
for (int i = 0; i < 3; i++) {
    for (int j = 0; j < 3; j++) {
        matrix[i][j] = scanner.nextInt();
    }
}

// Calculate the determinant of the matrix using Sarrus rule
int determinant = calculateDeterminantSarrus(matrix);

// Display the determinant of the matrix
System.out.println("Determinant of the matrix is: " +
determinant);

        scanner.close();
    }

    // Method to calculate the determinant of a 3x3 matrix using
Sarrus rule
    public static int calculateDeterminantSarrus(int[][] matrix) {
        int a = matrix[0][0];
        int b = matrix[0][1];
        int c = matrix[0][2];
        int d = matrix[1][0];
        int e = matrix[1][1];
        int f = matrix[1][2];
        int g = matrix[2][0];
        int h = matrix[2][1];
        int i = matrix[2][2];

        int determinant = (a * e * i) + (b * f * g) + (c * d * h) -
(c * e * g) - (a * f * h) - (b * d * i);
        return determinant;
    }
}
```

The rest of the program remains the same. We just updated the **calculateDeterminant()** method to use the Sarrus rule formula for finding the determinant.

88. Write a program that reads two matrices and returns the multiplication between them as an answer. The program should observe whether or not it is possible to perform the multiplication between the two matrices.

```java
import java.util.Scanner;

public class MatrixMultiplication {
    public static void main(String[] args) {
        Scanner scanner = new Scanner(System.in);

        // Read the dimensions of the first matrix
        System.out.println("Enter the dimensions of the first matrix
(rows columns):");
        int rows1 = scanner.nextInt();
        int columns1 = scanner.nextInt();

        // Read the dimensions of the second matrix
        System.out.println("Enter the dimensions of the second
matrix (rows columns):");
        int rows2 = scanner.nextInt();
        int columns2 = scanner.nextInt();

        if (columns1 != rows2) {
            System.out.println("Matrix multiplication is not
possible.");
            scanner.close();
            return;
        }

        // Create the first matrix and read its elements
        int[][] matrix1 = new int[rows1][columns1];
        System.out.println("Enter the elements of the first
matrix:");
        readMatrixElements(scanner, matrix1);

        // Create the second matrix and read its elements
        int[][] matrix2 = new int[rows2][columns2];
        System.out.println("Enter the elements of the second
matrix:");
        readMatrixElements(scanner, matrix2);

        // Multiply the two matrices and display the result
```

```java
        int[][] result = multiplyMatrices(matrix1, matrix2);
        System.out.println("Resulting Matrix:");
        displayMatrix(result);

        scanner.close();
    }

    // Method to read elements of a matrix from the user
    public static void readMatrixElements(Scanner scanner, int[][]
matrix) {
        for (int i = 0; i < matrix.length; i++) {
            for (int j = 0; j < matrix[0].length; j++) {
                matrix[i][j] = scanner.nextInt();
            }
        }
    }

    // Method to multiply two matrices
    public static int[][] multiplyMatrices(int[][] matrix1, int[][]
matrix2) {
        int rows1 = matrix1.length;
        int columns1 = matrix1[0].length;
        int rows2 = matrix2.length;
        int columns2 = matrix2[0].length;

        int[][] result = new int[rows1][columns2];

        for (int i = 0; i < rows1; i++) {
            for (int j = 0; j < columns2; j++) {
                for (int k = 0; k < columns1; k++) {
                    result[i][j] += matrix1[i][k] * matrix2[k][j];
                }
            }
        }

        return result;
    }

    // Method to display elements of a matrix
    public static void displayMatrix(int[][] matrix) {
        for (int i = 0; i < matrix.length; i++) {
            for (int j = 0; j < matrix[0].length; j++) {
                System.out.print(matrix[i][j] + "\t");
```

```
            }
            System.out.println();
        }
    }
}
```

Reading Matrix Dimensions:
The program starts by reading the dimensions of the two matrices from the user. The user is prompted to enter the number of rows and columns for each matrix. These dimensions are stored in variables *rows1*, *columns1* for the first matrix, and *rows2*, *columns2* for the second matrix.

Checking Matrix Compatibility:
Next, the program checks whether matrix multiplication is possible by comparing the number of columns in the first matrix (*columns1*) with the number of rows in the second matrix (*rows2*). If these two values are not equal, matrix multiplication cannot be performed, and the program displays a message saying that matrix multiplication is not possible. Then the program terminates.

Reading Matrix Elements:
If matrix multiplication is possible, the program proceeds to create two matrices *matrix1* and *matrix2* with the specified dimensions. It then prompts the user to enter the elements of each matrix. The *readMatrixElements()* method is used to read the elements of each matrix.

Matrix Multiplication:
After reading the elements of the two matrices, the program performs matrix multiplication using the *multiplyMatrices()* method. This method takes two matrices *matrix1* and *matrix2* as input and returns the resulting matrix as output. The multiplication is done by using three nested loops to iterate through each element of the resulting matrix and calculate its value based on the dot product of the corresponding rows and columns from the two input matrices.

Displaying the Result:
Finally, the program displays the resulting matrix using the *displayMatrix()* method. This method takes the resulting matrix as input and prints its elements row by row, separating each element with a tab (*t*) to format the output nicely.

89. Write a program that reads a 4x4 matrix and checks if it is a diagonal matrix, that is, if all elements outside the main diagonal are equal to zero.

```
import java.util.Scanner;
```

```java
public class DiagonalMatrixCheck {
    public static void main(String[] args) {
        Scanner scanner = new Scanner(System.in);

        // Create a 4x4 matrix
        int[][] matrix = new int[4][4];

        // Read the elements of the matrix from the user
        System.out.println("Enter the elements of the 4x4 matrix:");
        for (int i = 0; i < 4; i++) {
            for (int j = 0; j < 4; j++) {
                matrix[i][j] = scanner.nextInt();
            }
        }

        // Check if the matrix is a diagonal matrix
        boolean isDiagonalMatrix = true;
        for (int i = 0; i < 4; i++) {
            for (int j = 0; j < 4; j++) {
                // Check if the element is outside the main diagonal
                if (i != j && matrix[i][j] != 0) {
                    isDiagonalMatrix = false;
                    break;
                }
            }
            if (!isDiagonalMatrix) {
                break;
            }
        }

        // Display the result
        if (isDiagonalMatrix) {
            System.out.println("The matrix is a diagonal matrix.");
        } else {
            System.out.println("The matrix is not a diagonal
matrix.");
        }

        scanner.close();
    }
}
```

In this program, we start by creating a 4x4 matrix *matrix* to store the elements of the user's input. We then read the elements of the matrix from the user using nested loops.

Next, we use two nested loops to iterate through each element of the matrix and check if it is outside the main diagonal (i.e., *i != j*). If any element outside the main diagonal is found to be non-zero, we set the variable *isDiagonalMatrix* to *false*, indicating that the matrix is not a diagonal matrix. We use a boolean variable *isDiagonalMatrix* to keep track of whether all elements outside the main diagonal are equal to zero.

Finally, we display the result by checking the value of *isDiagonalMatrix*. If it is *true*, we print that the matrix is a diagonal matrix; otherwise, we print that the matrix is not a diagonal matrix.

90. Write a program that reads an m x n matrix, indicating the location where there are mines in a Minesweeper game (being 0 for a neutral field, and 1 for locations where there would be mines), and the program should return a matrix indicating, for each position, the number of mines in neighboring houses.

```java
import java.util.Scanner;

public class Minesweeper {
    public static void main(String[] args) {
        Scanner scanner = new Scanner(System.in);

        // Read the dimensions of the matrix
        System.out.print("Enter the number of rows (m): ");
        int m = scanner.nextInt();
        System.out.print("Enter the number of columns (n): ");
        int n = scanner.nextInt();

        // Create the minesweeper matrix
        int[][] minesweeperMatrix = new int[m][n];

        // Read the matrix indicating the locations of mines
        System.out.println("Enter the matrix indicating the
locations of mines (0 for neutral, 1 for mine):");
        for (int i = 0; i < m; i++) {
            for (int j = 0; j < n; j++) {
                minesweeperMatrix[i][j] = scanner.nextInt();
            }
        }

        // Create the matrix to store the counts of neighboring
```

mines
```
        int[][] minesCountMatrix = new int[m][n];

        // Calculate the number of mines in neighboring cells for
each position
        for (int i = 0; i < m; i++) {
            for (int j = 0; j < n; j++) {
                minesCountMatrix[i][j] =
countNeighboringMines(minesweeperMatrix, i, j, m, n);
            }
        }

        // Display the resulting matrix with the counts of
neighboring mines
        System.out.println("Matrix indicating the number of mines in
neighboring cells:");
        displayMatrix(minesCountMatrix);

        scanner.close();
    }

    // Method to calculate the number of mines in neighboring cells
for a given position
    public static int countNeighboringMines(int[][] matrix, int row,
int col, int m, int n) {
        int count = 0;

        // Define the eight possible directions to check for
neighboring cells
        int[] dx = { -1, -1, -1, 0, 0, 1, 1, 1 };
        int[] dy = { -1, 0, 1, -1, 1, -1, 0, 1 };

        // Check the eight neighboring cells
        for (int i = 0; i < 8; i++) {
            int newRow = row + dx[i];
            int newCol = col + dy[i];

            // Check if the new position is valid
            if (newRow >= 0 && newRow < m && newCol >= 0 && newCol <
n) {
                count += matrix[newRow][newCol];
            }
        }
```

```
        return count;
    }

    // Method to display a matrix
    public static void displayMatrix(int[][] matrix) {
        for (int[] row : matrix) {
            for (int cell : row) {
                System.out.print(cell + " ");
            }
            System.out.println();
        }
    }
}
```

The program starts by reading the dimensions **m** (number of rows) and **n** (number of columns) of the minesweeper matrix from the user.

Next, it creates the minesweeper matrix **minesweeperMatrix** and reads the values indicating the locations of mines from the user.

It then creates the **minesCountMatrix** to store the counts of neighboring mines for each position.

The program uses a nested loop to iterate through each position in the **minesCountMatrix**. For each position, it calls the **countNeighboringMines()** method to calculate the number of mines in neighboring cells. This method checks the eight adjacent cells using the **dx** and **dy** arrays to define the eight possible directions. It ensures that the new position is within the valid range of the matrix before counting the mines.

Finally, the program displays the **minesCountMatrix**, which indicates the number of mines in neighboring cells for each position.

Recursive Functions

91. Write a recursive function to calculate the factorial of a number.

```java
public class FactorialRecursive {
    public static void main(String[] args) {
        int number = 5;
        long factorial = calculateFactorial(number);
        System.out.println("Factorial of " + number + " is: " +
factorial);
    }

    public static long calculateFactorial(int n) {
        // Base case: factorial of 0 is 1
        if (n == 0) {
            return 1;
        } else {
            // Recursive call to calculate factorial of (n-1)
            return n * calculateFactorial(n - 1);
        }
    }
}
```

The function ***calculateFactorial()*** takes an integer n as input and returns a long integer (to handle larger factorials).

The base case of the recursive function is when ***n*** is 0. This is because the factorial of 0 is defined as 1 (0! = 1). When the function encounters ***n == 0***, it immediately returns 1.

If ***n*** is not 0, the function makes a recursive call to itself with the argument (***n-1***) to calculate the factorial of (***n-1***). This is the essence of the recursion. By breaking down the calculation into smaller subproblems (factorial of (***n-1***) in this case), the function can calculate the factorial of n by using the result of the factorial of (***n-1***).

The function will continue making recursive calls until it reaches the base case of ***n == 0***. At this point, the recursion will start to unwind, and each recursive call will return the factorial value back to the previous call.

92. Implement a recursive function to calculate the Fibonacci sequence up to a given number.

```java
import java.util.Arrays;

public class FibonacciRecursive {
    public static void main(String[] args) {
        int n = 10; // Replace this with the desired number
        int[] fibonacciSequence = calculateFibonacciSequence(n);
        System.out.println("Fibonacci sequence up to " + n + ": " +
Arrays.toString(fibonacciSequence));
    }

    public static int[] calculateFibonacciSequence(int n) {
        int[] fibonacci = new int[n + 1];
        for (int i = 0; i <= n; i++) {
            fibonacci[i] = fibonacciNumber(i);
        }
        return fibonacci;
    }

    public static int fibonacciNumber(int n) {
        if (n <= 1) {
            return n;
        } else {
            return fibonacciNumber(n - 1) + fibonacciNumber(n - 2);
        }
    }
}
```

The main function (*calculateFibonacciSequence()*) takes an integer *n* as input and returns an array containing the Fibonacci numbers up to *n*.

Inside the *calculateFibonacciSequence()* function, we create an integer array *fibonacci* of size *n + 1* to store the Fibonacci numbers.

We then use a for loop to fill the *fibonacci* array by calling the *fibonacciNumber()* function for each index *i* from 0 to *n*.

The *fibonacciNumber()* function is the recursive function that calculates the nth Fibonacci number. If *n* is less than or equal to 1, the function returns *n* directly because the first two Fibonacci numbers are 0 and 1. Otherwise, it calculates the Fibonacci number by making two recursive calls to calculate the (n-1)th and (n-2)th Fibonacci numbers and adds them together.

The *fibonacciNumber()* function will continue making recursive calls until it reaches the base case of *n <= 1*, at which point it returns *n* directly.

Finally, the main function returns the array *fibonacci*, containing the Fibonacci numbers up to the given number n.

93. Create a recursive function to check if a number is prime.

```java
public class PrimeRecursive {
    public static void main(String[] args) {
        int number = 17; // Replace this with the number you want to
check for primality
        boolean isPrime = isPrimeNumber(number);
        System.out.println(number + " is " + (isPrime ? "prime" :
"not prime"));
    }

    public static boolean isPrimeNumber(int n) {
        // Base cases: 0 and 1 are not prime, and 2 is the only even
prime number
        if (n <= 1) {
            return false;
        } else if (n == 2) {
            return true;
        }

        // Check for divisibility of n by numbers from 2 up to the
square root of n
        return isPrimeNumber(n, 2);
    }

    private static boolean isPrimeNumber(int n, int divisor) {
        // If the divisor reaches the square root of n or exceeds n,
n is prime
        if (divisor * divisor > n) {
            return true;
        }

        // If n is divisible by the current divisor, it is not prime
        if (n % divisor == 0) {
            return false;
        }

        // Check divisibility by the next odd divisor (divisor + 1)
        return isPrimeNumber(n, divisor + 1);
    }
}
```

The main function *isPrimeNumber()* takes an integer *n* as input and returns a boolean value indicating whether *n* is prime or not.

The base cases of the recursive function are:

- If **n** is less than or equal to 1, it is not prime (return **false**).
- If **n** is 2, it is the only even prime number (return **true**).

If n is greater than 2, the function calls the private helper function **isPrimeNumber(n, 2)** to perform the recursive check for primality.

The private helper function **isPrimeNumber(n, divisor)** is responsible for checking whether **n** is divisible by any number from 2 up to the square root of **n**. This is an optimization to reduce the number of iterations.

Inside the private helper function, it checks if **divisor * divisor > n**, which means it has already checked all possible divisors up to the square root of n. If this condition is met, the function returns **true**, indicating that **n** is prime.

If **n** is divisible by the current **divisor**, it means **n** is not prime, and the function returns **false**.

Otherwise, the function calls itself recursively with the next odd divisor (divisor + 1) to check divisibility by the next potential divisor.

94. Develop a recursive function to calculate the sum of the digits of an integer.

```
public class SumOfDigitsRecursive {
    public static void main(String[] args) {
        int number = 12345; // Replace this with the number for
which you want to calculate the sum of digits
        int sum = sumOfDigits(number);
        System.out.println("Sum of digits of " + number + " is: " +
sum);
    }

    public static int sumOfDigits(int number) {
        // Base case: If the number is a single digit, return the
number itself
        if (number < 10) {
            return number;
        }

        // Recursive step: Calculate the sum of the digits of the
number without its last digit
        int lastDigit = number % 10;
        int remainingDigits = number / 10;
        return lastDigit + sumOfDigits(remainingDigits);
    }
}
```

The main function **sumOfDigits()** takes an integer **number** as input and returns the sum of its digits.

The base case of the recursive function is when the **number** is a single-digit number (less than 10). In this case, the function directly returns the number itself, as the sum of its digits is equal to the number.

If the **number** is not a single-digit number, the function proceeds to the recursive step.

Inside the recursive step, the function calculates the last digit of the number (**lastDigit**) by taking the number modulo 10. It also calculates the remaining digits of the number (**remainingDigits**) by dividing the number by 10.

The function then makes a recursive call to itself with the argument **remainingDigits**. This recursive call calculates the sum of the digits of the number without its last digit.

Finally, the function returns the sum of the last digit and the sum of the digits of the remaining part of the number.

95. Write a recursive function to calculate the power of an integer raised to an exponent.

```
public class PowerRecursive {
    public static void main(String[] args) {
        int base = 2;
        int exponent = 5;
        int result = power(base, exponent);
        System.out.println(base + " raised to the power of " +
exponent + " is: " + result);
    }

    public static int power(int base, int exponent) {
        // Base case: If the exponent is 0, return 1 (any number
raised to the power of 0 is 1)
        if (exponent == 0) {
            return 1;
        }

        // Recursive step: Calculate the power of the base raised to
the (exponent - 1)
        int result = base * power(base, exponent - 1);
        return result;
    }
}
```

The main function **power()** takes two integers **base** and **exponent** as input and returns the result of **base** raised to the power of **exponent**.

The base case of the recursive function is when the **exponent** is 0. In this case, the function directly returns 1 because any number raised to the power of 0 is 1.

If the **exponent** is not 0, the function proceeds to the recursive step.

Inside the recursive step, the function makes a recursive call to itself with the arguments **base** and **exponent - 1**. This recursive call calculates the power of the base raised to the (exponent - 1).

Finally, the function returns the result of multiplying **base** with the power of the base raised to the (exponent - 1).

96. Implement a recursive function to find the greatest common divisor (GCD) of two numbers.

```java
public class GCDRecursive {
    public static void main(String[] args) {
        int number1 = 48;
        int number2 = 18;
        int gcd = findGCD(number1, number2);
        System.out.println("GCD of " + number1 + " and " + number2 +
" is: " + gcd);
    }

    public static int findGCD(int a, int b) {
        // Base case: If one of the numbers is 0, return the other
number as GCD
        if (b == 0) {
            return a;
        }

        // Recursive step: Calculate the GCD of b and the remainder
when a is divided by b
        return findGCD(b, a % b);
    }
}
```

The main function **findGCD()** takes two integers **a** and **b** as input and returns their greatest common divisor (GCD).

The base case of the recursive function is when **b** is 0. In this case, the GCD is **a** itself. We return **a** as the result.

If **b** is not 0, the function proceeds to the recursive step.

Inside the recursive step, the function makes a recursive call to itself with the arguments **b** and the remainder when **a** is divided by **b**. This is done using the modulus operator (**%**), which calculates the remainder of the division.

The recursive call continues until b becomes 0, and at that point, the function returns **a**, which is the GCD of the two numbers.

97. Create a recursive function to reverse a string.

```java
public class StringReversalRecursive {
    public static void main(String[] args) {
        String input = "Hello, World!";
        String reversed = reverseString(input);
        System.out.println("Original String: " + input);
        System.out.println("Reversed String: " + reversed);
    }

    public static String reverseString(String str) {
        // Base case: If the string has only one character or is
empty, return the string itself
        if (str.length() <= 1) {
            return str;
        }

        // Recursive step: Concatenate the last character with the
reversed substring (excluding the last character)
        char lastChar = str.charAt(str.length() - 1);
        String substring = str.substring(0, str.length() - 1);
        return lastChar + reverseString(substring);
    }
}
```

The main function ***reverseString()*** takes a string ***str*** as input and returns the reversed string.

The base case of the recursive function is when the length of the string ***str*** is 1 or less. In this case, the function directly returns the string itself, as a single-character string or an empty string is its own reverse.

If the string ***str*** has more than one character, the function proceeds to the recursive step.

Inside the recursive step, the function extracts the last character (***lastChar***) of the string using the ***charAt()*** method.

It also extracts the substring of ***str*** excluding the last character using the ***substring()*** method.

The function then makes a recursive call to itself with the substring as the argument. This recursive call reverses the substring.

Finally, the function concatenates the last character with the reversed substring and returns the resulting string as the reversed string of the original input.

98. Develop a recursive function to find the smallest value in an array.

```
public class SmallestValueRecursive {
    public static void main(String[] args) {
        int[] array = {5, 2, 8, 1, 7, 3};
        int smallest = findSmallestValue(array);
        System.out.println("The smallest value in the array is: " +
smallest);
    }

    public static int findSmallestValue(int[] arr) {
        return findSmallestValueRecursive(arr, 0,
Integer.MAX_VALUE);
    }

    private static int findSmallestValueRecursive(int[] arr, int
index, int currentSmallest) {
        // Base case: If we have reached the end of the array,
return the current smallest value
        if (index == arr.length) {
            return currentSmallest;
        }

        // Recursive step: Compare the current element with the
current smallest value
        // Update the current smallest value if necessary
        currentSmallest = Math.min(currentSmallest, arr[index]);

        // Make a recursive call to process the next element in the
array
        return findSmallestValueRecursive(arr, index + 1,
currentSmallest);
    }
}
```

The main function *findSmallestValue()* takes an integer array *arr* as input and returns the smallest value in the array.

The *findSmallestValue()* function simply calls the private helper function *findSmallestValueRecursive()* with the initial index 0 and the initial value of *currentSmallest* set to *Integer.MAX_VALUE*.

The private helper function *findSmallestValueRecursive()* takes three arguments: the integer array *arr*, the current index *index*, and the current smallest value *currentSmallest*.

The base case of the recursive function is when the **index** reaches the length of the array, which means we have processed all elements. In this case, the function returns the current smallest value.

Inside the recursive step, the function compares the current element at index **arr[index]** with the current smallest value **currentSmallest**. It updates the **currentSmallest** to the smaller of the two values using **Math.min()**.

The function then makes a recursive call to itself with the next index **index + 1** and the updated **currentSmallest**.

The recursive calls continue until all elements in the array have been processed, and the function finally returns the smallest value found.

99. Write a recursive function to determine whether a word is a palindrome.

```java
public class PalindromeRecursive {
    public static void main(String[] args) {
        String word1 = "level";
        String word2 = "hello";

        System.out.println(word1 + " is a palindrome? " +
isPalindrome(word1));
        System.out.println(word2 + " is a palindrome? " +
isPalindrome(word2));
    }

    public static boolean isPalindrome(String word) {
        // Base case: If the word is empty or has only one
character, it is a palindrome
        if (word.length() <= 1) {
            return true;
        }

        // Compare the first and last characters
        if (word.charAt(0) != word.charAt(word.length() - 1)) {
            return false; // The word is not a palindrome
        }

        // Recursive step: Check the substring without the first and
last characters
        String subWord = word.substring(1, word.length() - 1);
        return isPalindrome(subWord);
    }
}
```

The main function ***isPalindrome()*** takes a string ***word*** as input and returns ***true*** if the word is a palindrome and ***false*** otherwise.

The base case of the recursive function is when the length of the word is 0 or 1. In this case, the function directly returns ***true*** because an empty string or a single-character string is always a palindrome.

If the word has more than one character, the function proceeds to the recursive step.

Inside the recursive step, the function compares the first character ***word.charAt(0)*** with the last character ***word.charAt(word.length() - 1)*** of the word.

If the first and last characters are not equal, it means the word is not a palindrome, and the function returns ***false***.

If the first and last characters are equal, the function creates a substring ***subWord*** without the first and last characters using the ***substring()*** method.

The function then makes a recursive call to itself with the ***subWord*** as the argument. This recursive call continues the palindrome check with the remaining substring.

The recursive calls continue until a mismatch is found, or the word becomes empty or has only one character. If all characters are matched during the recursion, the function returns ***true***, indicating that the word is a palindrome.

100. Implement a recursive function to calculate the sum of elements of an array.

```java
public class ArraySumRecursive {
    public static void main(String[] args) {
        int[] array = {2, 4, 6, 8, 10};
        int sum = calculateSum(array);
        System.out.println("Sum of elements in the array: " + sum);
    }

    public static int calculateSum(int[] arr) {
        return calculateSumRecursive(arr, arr.length - 1);
    }

    private static int calculateSumRecursive(int[] arr, int index) {
        // Base case: If the index is negative (no more elements to
add), return 0
        if (index < 0) {
            return 0;
        }

        // Recursive step: Add the current element to the sum of the
remaining elements
```

```
        int currentElement = arr[index];
        return currentElement + calculateSumRecursive(arr, index -
1);
    }
}
```

The main function **calculateSum()** takes an integer array **arr** as input and returns the sum of elements in the array.

The **calculateSum()** function simply calls the private helper function **calculateSumRecursive()** with the initial **index** set to **arr.length - 1**.

The private helper function **calculateSumRecursive()** takes two arguments: the integer array **arr** and the current **index**.

The base case of the recursive function is when the **index** becomes negative, which means we have no more elements to add. In this case, the function returns 0.

Inside the recursive step, the function calculates the sum by adding the current element at index **arr[index]** to the sum of the remaining elements. The remaining elements' sum is obtained by making a recursive call with the index decremented by 1.

The recursive calls continue until all elements in the array have been added to the sum, and the function finally returns the sum of the elements.

Extra Exercises

101. Write a program that prompts the user for a sentence and displays the sentence backwards

```java
import java.util.Scanner;

public class SentenceReverser {
    public static void main(String[] args) {
        Scanner scanner = new Scanner(System.in);

        System.out.print("Enter a sentence: ");
        String sentence = scanner.nextLine();

        String reversedSentence = reverseSentence(sentence);
        System.out.println("Reversed sentence: " +
reversedSentence);

        scanner.close();
    }

    public static String reverseSentence(String sentence) {
        String[] words = sentence.split(" ");
        StringBuilder reversed = new StringBuilder();

        for (int i = words.length - 1; i >= 0; i--) {
            reversed.append(words[i]).append(" ");
        }

        return reversed.toString().trim();
    }
}
```

The program begins by creating a **Scanner** object to read the user input.

The user is prompted to enter a sentence using **System.out.print("Enter a sentence: ")**, and the input is read using **scanner.nextLine()**.

The **reverseSentence()** function takes the input **sentence** as an argument and returns the reversed sentence as a **String**.

Inside the **reverseSentence()** function, we split the input sentence into an array of words using **sentence.split(" ")**.

We use a **StringBuilder** named **reversed** to build the reversed sentence.

In the **for** loop, we iterate through the words array in reverse order (from the last word to the first word) and append each word, followed by a space, to the **reversed** StringBuilder.

After the loop finishes, we use **reversed.toString().trim()** to convert the **StringBuilder** into a **String** and remove any leading or trailing spaces.

The reversed sentence is returned to the **main()** function.

Finally, the program prints the reversed sentence using **System.out.println("Reversed sentence: " + reversedSentence)**.

102. Make the BubbleSort Algorithm

The Bubble Sort algorithm is a simple sorting algorithm that repeatedly steps through the list, compares adjacent elements, and swaps them if they are in the wrong order. The algorithm continues to pass through the list until the entire list is sorted. Here's the implementation of the Bubble Sort algorithm in Java:

```java
public class BubbleSort {
    public static void main(String[] args) {
        int[] arr = {64, 34, 25, 12, 22, 11, 90};

        System.out.println("Original Array:");
        printArray(arr);

        bubbleSort(arr);

        System.out.println("Sorted Array:");
        printArray(arr);
    }

    public static void bubbleSort(int[] arr) {
        int n = arr.length;
        boolean swapped;

        for (int i = 0; i < n - 1; i++) {
            swapped = false;

            for (int j = 0; j < n - i - 1; j++) {
                if (arr[j] > arr[j + 1]) {
                    // Swap arr[j] and arr[j+1]
                    int temp = arr[j];
                    arr[j] = arr[j + 1];
                    arr[j + 1] = temp;
                    swapped = true;
                }
```

```
        }

            // If no two elements were swapped in the inner loop,
the array is already sorted
            if (!swapped) {
                break;
            }
        }
    }

    public static void printArray(int[] arr) {
        for (int i = 0; i < arr.length; i++) {
            System.out.print(arr[i] + " ");
        }
        System.out.println();
    }
}
```

The *main* method initializes an integer array *arr* with some values and prints the original array.

The *bubbleSort* method implements the Bubble Sort algorithm.

The outer loop runs from *i = 0* to *i = n - 1*, where *n* is the length of the array.

The inner loop runs from *j = 0* to *j = n - i - 1*.

For each pair of adjacent elements *arr[j]* and *arr[j + 1]*, if *arr[j]* is greater than *arr[j + 1]*, the two elements are swapped to bring the larger element towards the end of the array.

After each pass of the outer loop, the largest element in the unsorted part of the array "bubbles up" to the correct position.

The algorithm repeats this process until the entire array is sorted.

The *printArray* method is used to display the array.

103. Make an algorithm that solves the Tower of Hanoi

The Tower of Hanoi is a classic mathematical puzzle that consists of three rods and a number of disks of different sizes, which can slide onto any rod. The puzzle starts with the disks in a stack on one rod in ascending order of size, with the smallest disk at the top. The objective is to move the entire stack to another rod, following these rules:
- Only one disk can be moved at a time.
- Each move consists of taking the upper disk from one of the stacks and placing it on top of another stack or on an empty rod.
- No disk may be placed on top of a smaller disk.

Here's a recursive algorithm to solve the Tower of Hanoi puzzle in Java:
public class TowerOfHanoi {

```java
public static void main(String[] args) {
    int numDisks = 3; // Number of disks
    char sourcePeg = 'A'; // Source peg
    char auxiliaryPeg = 'B'; // Auxiliary peg
    char destinationPeg = 'C'; // Destination peg

    solveTowerOfHanoi(numDisks, sourcePeg, auxiliaryPeg,
destinationPeg);
    }

    public static void solveTowerOfHanoi(int n, char source, char
auxiliary, char destination) {
        if (n == 1) {
            System.out.println("Move disk 1 from " + source + " to "
+ destination);
            return;
        }

        // Move (n-1) disks from source to auxiliary peg using
destination peg
        solveTowerOfHanoi(n - 1, source, destination, auxiliary);

        // Move the nth disk from source to destination peg
        System.out.println("Move disk " + n + " from " + source + "
to " + destination);

        // Move (n-1) disks from auxiliary peg to destination peg
using source peg
        solveTowerOfHanoi(n - 1, auxiliary, source, destination);
    }
}
```

Let's break down the algorithm step by step:

The main method initializes the number of disks (***numDisks***) and the pegs (***sourcePeg, auxiliaryPeg, destinationPeg***) as characters 'A', 'B', and 'C', respectively.

The ***solveTowerOfHanoi*** method is a recursive function that takes four arguments:

- ***n***: The number of disks to be moved.
- ***source***: The peg from which the disks need to be moved.
- ***auxiliary***: The peg to be used as an auxiliary for moving the disks.
- ***destination***: The peg where the disks need to be moved.

166

The base case of the recursion is when **n** is 1. In this case, there is only one disk to be moved, and it is directly moved from the source peg to the destination peg.

In the recursive step, we first move (n-1) disks from the source peg to the auxiliary peg using the destination peg as an auxiliary.

Then, we move the nth disk from the source peg to the destination peg.

Finally, we recursively move (n-1) disks from the auxiliary peg to the destination peg using the source peg as an auxiliary.

The algorithm repeats this process until all the disks are moved to the destination peg.

104. Make a function that receives a 3x3 matrix representing the game of tic-tac-toe, and check if there is a winner, if there is a tie, or if the game is not over yet.

```java
public class TicTacToe {
    public static void main(String[] args) {
        int[][] board = {
            {1, 1, 2},
            {2, 2, 1},
            {1, 0, 0}
        };

        int result = checkGameStatus(board);
        if (result == 0) {
            System.out.println("The game is still ongoing.");
        } else if (result == 1) {
            System.out.println("Player 1 is the winner.");
        } else if (result == 2) {
            System.out.println("Player 2 is the winner.");
        } else {
            System.out.println("The game is a tie.");
        }
    }

    public static int checkGameStatus(int[][] board) {
        // Check rows
        for (int row = 0; row < 3; row++) {
            if (board[row][0] != 0 && board[row][0] == board[row][1]
 && board[row][1] == board[row][2]) {
                return board[row][0];
            }
        }
```

```
        // Check columns
        for (int col = 0; col < 3; col++) {
            if (board[0][col] != 0 && board[0][col] == board[1][col]
&& board[1][col] == board[2][col]) {
                return board[0][col];
            }
        }

        // Check diagonals
        if (board[0][0] != 0 && board[0][0] == board[1][1] &&
board[1][1] == board[2][2]) {
            return board[0][0];
        }
        if (board[0][2] != 0 && board[0][2] == board[1][1] &&
board[1][1] == board[2][0]) {
            return board[0][2];
        }

        // Check if the game is still ongoing
        for (int row = 0; row < 3; row++) {
            for (int col = 0; col < 3; col++) {
                if (board[row][col] == 0) {
                    return 0; // The game is still ongoing
                }
            }
        }

        // If no winner and no empty cells, it's a tie
        return -1;
    }
}
```

The **checkGameStatus** function takes a 3x3 integer array **board** representing the Tic-Tac-Toe game as input.

The function first checks for a winning condition by iterating through each row, column, and both diagonals.

If any row, column, or diagonal has all the same non-zero value (1 for player 1, 2 for player 2), it means there is a winner, and the function returns the winning player's number.

If no winner is found, the function checks if there are any empty cells left in the board. If there are, it means the game is still ongoing, and the function returns 0.

If there are no empty cells left and no winner, it means the game is a tie, and the function returns -1.

The main method demonstrates how to use the ***checkGameStatus***
function with a sample 3x3 matrix representing a Tic-Tac-Toe game. It prints
the result of the game, whether it's still ongoing, or if there's a winner or a tie.

105. Rawwords: Write an algorithm that checks whether a word is a "rawword". A word is considered a "prime word" if the sum of the letter values (where 'a' = 1, 'b' = 2, etc.) is a prime number.

To check whether a word is a "rawword" (a prime word), we can write an
algorithm that calculates the sum of the letter values in the word and then
checks if the sum is a prime number. Here's a step-by-step algorithm to
accomplish this:

```java
public class RawwordChecker {
    public static void main(String[] args) {
        String word = "Hello";
        if (isRawWord(word)) {
            System.out.println(word + " is a rawword.");
        } else {
            System.out.println(word + " is not a rawword.");
        }
    }

    public static boolean isRawWord(String word) {
        int sum = 0;
        for (char c : word.toCharArray()) {
            sum += getLetterValue(c);
        }
        return isPrime(sum);
    }

    public static boolean isPrime(int n) {
        if (n <= 1) {
            return false;
        }
        for (int i = 2; i <= Math.sqrt(n); i++) {
            if (n % i == 0) {
                return false;
            }
        }
        return true;
    }

    public static int getLetterValue(char c) {
```

```
        return Character.toLowerCase(c) - 'a' + 1;
    }
}
```

The **isPrime** method checks if a number n is prime. It returns *false* if *n* is less than or equal to 1. Then, it iterates from 2 to the square root of *n* and checks if *n* is divisible by any number in that range. If it finds a divisor, it returns *false*; otherwise, it returns *true*.

The **getLetterValue** method calculates the letter value of a character *c* by converting it to lowercase, subtracting the ASCII value of 'a', and adding 1.

The **isRawWord** method takes a word as input and calculates the sum of the letter values using the **getLetterValue** method. Then, it checks if the sum is a prime number using the **isPrime** method. If the sum is prime, the method returns *true*, indicating that the word is a "rawword"; otherwise, it returns *false*.

The **main** method tests the algorithm with the word "Hello" and prints whether it is a "rawword" or not.

106. Implement an algorithm that takes an integer and generates the Collatz sequence for that number. The Collatz sequence is generated by applying the following rules: if the number is even, divide it by 2; if the number is odd, multiply it by 3 and add 1. Repeat this process until you reach the number 1.

```java
import java.util.ArrayList;

public class CollatzSequence {
    public static void main(String[] args) {
        int number = 20;
        ArrayList<Integer> sequence =
generateCollatzSequence(number);

        System.out.println("Collatz Sequence for " + number + ":");
        for (int num : sequence) {
            System.out.print(num + " ");
        }
    }

    public static ArrayList<Integer> generateCollatzSequence(int
number) {
        ArrayList<Integer> sequence = new ArrayList<>();
        sequence.add(number);
```

```
    while (number != 1) {
        if (number % 2 == 0) {
            number = number / 2;
        } else {
            number = number * 3 + 1;
        }
        sequence.add(number);
    }

    return sequence;
    }
}
```

The **generateCollatzSequence** method takes an integer **number** as input and returns an **ArrayList** of integers representing the Collatz sequence for that number.

We start by creating an **ArrayList** called **sequence** to store the numbers in the Collatz sequence. We add the initial number (**number**) to the **sequence** list.

We use a while loop to keep generating the next numbers in the sequence until we reach the number 1. In each iteration, we apply the rules of the Collatz sequence:

- If the current number is even (**number % 2 == 0**), we divide it by 2 (**number = number / 2**).
- If the current number is odd, we multiply it by 3 and add 1 (**number = number * 3 + 1**).

We add each newly generated number to the **sequence** list in each iteration.

When the loop reaches the number 1, the Collatz sequence generation is complete, and the method returns the **sequence** list containing all the numbers in the sequence.

The **main** method tests the algorithm with the number 20 and prints the Collatz sequence for that number.

Complete List of Exercises

Additional Content

In case you want to access the code of all the exercises, you can get it from the link below:

https://forms.gle/Tjk7GR435Ed5fJJV8

Each file is named with the exercise number, with the extension .java

About the Author

Ruhan Avila da Conceição (@ruhanconceicao, on social media) holds a degree in Computer Engineering (2015) from the Federal University of Pelotas and a Master's in Computing (2016) also from the same university. Since 2018 he has been a professor at the Federal Institute of Education, Science and Technology in the field of Informatics, where he teaches, among others, the disciplines of Object Oriented Programming, Visual Programming and Mobile Device Programming.

In 2014, even as an undergraduate student, Ruhan received the title of Researcher from Rio Grande do Sul in the Young Innovator category due to his academic and scientific career during his years at the university. His research topic has always been related to the algorithmic development of efficient solutions for encoding videos in real time. Still with regard to scientific research, Ruhan accumulates dozens of works published in national and international congresses, as well as articles in scientific journals of great relevance, and two computer programs registered at the National Institute of Intellectual Property.

Initiated in programming in the C language, Ruhan Conceição has extensive knowledge in JavaScript languages, as well as their libraries and frameworks ReactJS, React Native, NextJS; and Java. In addition, the author has also developed projects in Python, C#, Matlab, GoogleScript and C++.

Mastering Python

Mastering Python: 100+ Solved and Commented Exercises to Accelerate Your Learning

www.ingramcontent.com/pod-product-compliance
Lightning Source LLC
LaVergne TN
LVHW081526050326
832903LV00025B/1652